Born With a Rusty Spoon

an artist's memoir

Bertie Stroup Marah

Plain View Press
P.O. 42255
Austin, TX 78704

plainviewpress.net
sb@plainviewpress.net
512-441-2452

ISBN: 978-1-935514-66-4
Library of Congress Number: 2010927911

Cover art: Bertie Stroup Marah
Cover design by Susan Bright

This book is dedicated to Willie and Reita
and the memory of Jessie and Phyllis

Bertie and dolls in brother's wagon

Chapter One

I wasn't mad at my mama, nor was I spiteful. I just wanted her attention. In my three-year-old mind, the best way to get it was to pee my pants. She would then be forced to turn her attention from starting a fire in the wood cook stove to changing my soiled underpants.

I had felt slighted earlier that morning when she slipped from our warm bed and whispered, "Bertie, you just stay warm and snug while I run next door to borrow some coffee from Rosalee." Rosalee lived in a little two-room house that was a duplicate of our own barren living quarters. Rosalee was almost as beautiful as Mama, but unlike Mama, who was just twenty-three and already had three children, Rosalee had none. I was jealous of any time Mama spent at her house because the minutes seemed like hours when she was away.

"But Mama, I want to go too," I whined.

"No, I'll only be a minute. You stay right here." She pulled the door firmly shut as she left. I lay there looking at the stains on the ceiling and studying the torn wallpaper that had been patched with cardboard in places. Even at the young age of three, my creative self was intrigued by the shapes of the roses and leaves on the faded wallpaper. I considered just peeing in the bed but because Mama knew I was awake she would never believe it was an accident. I wished she would hurry up and come back as I wiggled my toes and waited impatiently for the door to open. She loves me, I thought, so maybe she'll hug me and say she's sorry when she sees how sad I am. She ignored my pouting when she returned to start a breakfast of biscuits and gravy. That's all we would have this morning. Yesterday my brother, Jessie, had used a biscuit to sop the last of the syrup from the Brer Rabbit Syrup can.

My two brothers slept in the other room of our two-room house and Mama and I slept on a bed in the same room as the cook stove and table. As she dipped water from a bucket and poured it into the coffee pot I slid out of bed onto the rough planked floor and stood staring at her back. She seemed to take no notice of me.

My plan to gain her attention took shape as I watched her stir the biscuit dough. She had scraped the dough onto the flour scattered on the table top and was beginning to knead it when I quietly backed to the door and slipped outside. I squatted, and proceeded with the messy task of deliberately wetting my pants. I was intently studying the growing pattern of the little flood I was creating between my feet when I was startled by the sound of footsteps coming around the corner of the house. I looked up to see my seven-year-old brother, Willie, walking along the path from a visit to the outhouse. Willie stopped in his tracks as his eyebrows shot up in surprise then lowered and squinted into a frown when he realized what I was up to.

"Bertie, what do you think you're doin'?" he scolded. "Only babies pee their pants."

Willie was my hero as far back as I can remember. Some people are just born good and being so comes naturally to them. Willie is one of those people. He was very responsible for his age and helped Mama look after my five-year-old brother, Jessie, and me much of the time.

"I didn't mean to, my pants got stuck," I whimpered as tears filled my eyes. "Don't tell Mama, please don't tell Mama."

Willie led me, still dripping, back inside. "Mama, look what I caught Bertie doin'."

I stared at my pee splattered feet and Mama scolded, "Shame on you, Bertie." She handed me a clean pair of underpants from an old trunk in the corner where we kept our clean clothes. "I think you're big enough to change your own dirty britches now."

Realizing I had used a rather indefensible act in order to gain my mother's attention, I ducked my head and muttered, "I won't do it any more, Mama." Even as the words left my lips I was trying to develop a more sophisticated means to achieve my goal. My change in strategy would include a bonus of relief from a chapped butt and offensive odor.

I was too young to realize that at the time Mama was struggling with a failing marriage to my daddy who was away most of the time on his job as a trapper. She was doing her best in his absence to take care of my older brothers and me while living in a two-room house with no electricity and no indoor plumbing. The house was located near the middle of the tiny village of Weed, New Mexico. In addition to her personal stressful situation, World War II had just started, bringing with it the military draft as well as the rationing of gas, tires, cooking oil, sugar and other necessities. Talk of the war was a favorite subject in those times and I was too young to understand most of it. I once said to Mama, "Mr. Hitler must be a very bad man, why is he so mean?"

She sighed, "Some people just never seem to have enough; they always want more."

"Well," I said while staring at the empty sugar jar, "I sure wish we could have more."

I'm sure she did too. It had been two weeks since Daddy had been home to give her money for groceries. She and Rosalee were sitting at our kitchen table the night before when I overheard Mama say, "I guess I'll try to get some groceries on credit down at Goss's store 'til Hollan comes home. I hate to ask. We just got him paid off from the last time. Besides, me and Hollan have been havin' some more trouble lately and I'm not sure when he is gonna make it home."

I didn't like the worried tone in her voice and figured she didn't say more because I was listening. Then it got quiet and Mama said, "Watch out for big ears on little children."

A couple of days later, we awoke to a rainy morning that continued into a gray afternoon so we couldn't go outside to play as we usually did. We had few toys and after awhile we got tired of cutting things out of the Sears catalogue. We were bored with our confinement. Mama gave us a bowl of pinto beans and cold biscuits for lunch then sat quietly patching the boys' pants with a needle and thread. She sang softly the tune to Jimmy Roger's old song about a lonesome hobo. Sad songs were especially popular at that time following the Great Depression. Mama had a beautiful voice that sounded especially sad that day. She may have been thinking about Daddy or maybe the rain just had her feeling blue.

Sensing our restlessness, Mama repeated the same thing she had told us earlier that morning, "I think your daddy will be home today, if he don't get stuck in the mud somewhere." Each time she had a hopeful note in her voice.

Jessie loved Daddy to distraction and missed him every minute he was away. Her promise was all it took for Jessie to run back and forth to the window where he pressed his nose to the glass. "When, Mama, when do think he'll be here. Will it be before dark?"

"I don't know Jessie, we'll just have to wait and see. And stop askin' every five minutes."

Willie was attempting to repair his slingshot with a strip of rubber he had cut from an old discarded inner tube. A half-hearted squabble erupted between Jessie and me. Mama broke it up with another promise of Daddy coming home. We then stood at the window watching raindrops make their way to the bottom of the pane. The rain turned the usually dry ravine that ran through the village near our house into a flowing stream of muddy water. The sight of the rushing water fascinated us.

"Do you want to go swimmin'?" I whispered to Jessie.

He hesitated. "I don't think Mama wants us to."

I leaned close to him, looking directly into his pale blue eyes. "Oh she won't care."

After a moment he nodded. "O.K., but I don't have a swim suit."

I thought for a moment. "We don't need any. Let's just wear our underpants."

Our excitement mounted at the prospect of wading in the muddy water that now raced through the ravine. Hidden from Mama's view, we slipped out the back door.

"Hurry up, Jessie," I urged as I tucked the bottom of my dress into the top of my panties.

"Do you think anyone will see my underpants?" Jessie asked worriedly.

"No, just hurry up!"

We stepped into the water and goose bumps immediately appeared on our arms. "Boy, this is cold," Jessie said.

"Yeah, and I can't walk very good." I struggled to maintain my footing.

We waded in far enough that the swirling water hit our thighs and our footing was becoming less sure. I grabbed Jessie's arm to keep from falling. We were laughing and splashing and did not hear Willie yelling. "Mama, come here! They're in the creek."

Our good time came to an abrupt halt when over the rushing water we heard Mama's terrified voice, "No, no," she screamed, "my God, stop!"

Her terrified shriek startled me and my feet slipped out from under me just as she grabbed my hand. She dragged us by the arms to the muddy bank, shouting every slippery step of the way. Her continued scolding stung but her words contrasted with what her embrace told us as she knelt and held us tightly.

"Don't ever do somethin' like that again," she said in a shaking voice. "What would I ever do without my babies?"

We returned shivering to the house where Mama washed and dressed us in clean clothes. We continued our vigil in anticipation of Daddy's return home. We could not have imagined that his return would end in heartbreak for us all.

Bertie and her brothers Willie and Jessie (ages 3, 7, and 5 respectively)

Chapter Two

*W*e accepted Mama's strength and love as a given. It is in hindsight that we realized her determination and strong attitudes were shaped by the hardships that came early in life.

My mother was born near Muskogee, Oklahoma in 1919 as Felia Beatrice Counts, a name that she detested and later changed to just plain 'Bee' Counts. She was second in a family of six children, born between an older and younger brother. Her family was poor and her father earned what he could by share cropping and carpentry.

When she was five years old the family lived on an old run-down farm in Oklahoma. She and her older brother, Horace and younger brother, Dick, were in the loft of the barn eating green peanuts. This was in direct defiance of their mother's orders. Just that morning she had warned, "Now, don't go eatin' anymore of those green peanuts, they'll give you the runs again." They made every effort to avoid discovery and stayed as quiet as they could as they stuffed the forbidden peanuts into their mouths. They certainly couldn't risk crawling down from the loft when they felt the desperate need to pee. The sensible decision was clearly to pee where they were.

As Horace and Dick approached the opening in the front of the loft to relieve themselves, Horace, recognized the opportunity to play a game he was sure to win, and said, "Dick, I bet I can pee further than you." With a giggle, Dick unbuttoned his overalls and challenged, "Let 'er rip," thereby entering the competition. Bee, who never wanted to be outdone cried out, "Me too," as she lifted her skirt jerked her underpants off, pushed her pelvis forward and proceeded to empty her bladder by peeing as far as she could.

The result was nothing she could have foreseen; a little stream of her pee dripped through the crack in the floor and onto her father's head as he was milking a cow in the stall below.

"What in the hell?" Grandpa yelled. "You kids get down here right now." Although Bee was punished in accordance with the degree of her peanut transgression and unlady-like behavior, she never got over the urge to accept physical challenges. The fact is her whole life could be summed up as one continuous "pissing contest," especially where the opposite sex was concerned.

In his younger days, Bee's father, Jack Counts, was a tall handsome man whose own father ruled his family with an iron fist. After the family moved from Missouri to Oklahoma, Jack liked to go to Indian powwow dances just to watch. It was there he met his first wife, a Choctaw Indian woman. Great Grandpa Counts thought she was probably rich from the oil royalties of her native land. He insisted Jack marry her.

"You marry that Indian woman and you won't ever have to worry about money again, Jackson," he assured his son.

A few weeks after exchanging vows, the honeymoon along with his libido, were becoming faded memories. At that point, Jack insisted that he take over their finances. This didn't sit well with his wife and she soon discovered that Jack had married her for her money. The marriage didn't last long after that. She drove him in her buggy to the banks of the Canadian River where she held a gun on him. Her dark eyes were black with rage. His had turned round with fear.

"Jack, get out of this buggy," she ordered. If you can swim to the other side of that river with me shootin' at you, you get to live."

Knowing she meant business, he ran zigzagging to the river dodging bullets. He was a good swimmer and would later say as he shook his head with a sigh of relief, "I felt damned lucky not to have been turned into a sieve."

A few years later he met and married my grandma Bertie, whom he adored. He remained loyal to her for the rest of his life even when she changed. She was so lovely and sweet when he first met her that he could not imagine living without her. Perhaps those memories were what kept him in love with her when, after years of hardship and child bearing, her tongue became as sharp as a knife. She ignored him, blaming him for her unhappiness. He rarely addressed her by her given name. Instead he used endearing pet names. However, all his "sugarpots," "sweethearts" and "darlins," cloaked in steadfast love, fell on deaf ears.

Grandpa was a very musical man who danced and sang beautifully. He played the harmonica too, before asthma stole his breath. Grandma was quick to take credit for their musically talented children, but her lack of rhythm denied this claim. She could not keep time and danced no better than a hobbled horse. Her singing was not very good, and time had no positive influence on it.

Jackson Counts, Bertie's grandfather around the time he married for money

During the Great Depression and dust bowl days Mama's family was part of the migration from Oklahoma that forced poor families to leave the state in search of work. From Oklahoma their first move was to the oil field town of Borger, Texas where Grandpa ran a small grocery store. He scratched together enough money to sparsely stock the shelves of a rundown old building he rented. Times were tough and he wasn't a very good business man. Being both generous and impractical, he went broke from extending too much credit to desperate families.

In March of 1933, they packed their belongings in the back of their old Model A and headed farther west into New Mexico. The truck's old four-cylinder engine had a lot of wear and the tires were worn smooth. It was fortunate that the roads were mostly flat for on sharp inclines the old truck, loaded as it was, didn't have the power to make it over the top. To lighten the load they would sometimes get out and push the sluggish vehicle up the hill. They camped along the highways, cooked over an open fire, and slept on the ground. At every stop they asked for work. Some of the people they talked to were sympathetic when they saw this rag-tag bunch while it seemed that a few had to make an effort to hide their disdain. Perhaps these pious few thought they had brought their misfortune upon themselves.

They were camping outside of Corona, New Mexico when an old rancher came by and offered them shelter.

"It ain't got no windows or doors, but it will be a roof over your head and you won't have to sleep on the ground. The only thing is, this place is crawling with rattlesnakes so you'll have to watch out for 'em." The old rancher pushed back his dirty old hat, spit out a chew of tobacco and scratched his scaly scalp.

"I don't have much money, but if you want to build fencing for a day or two I can probably help you out with a few groceries and some gas."

"I appreciate that very much," Grandpa said, "and I'll take you up on your offer." He turned to his oldest son, Horace, "Son, it's gettin' dark, why don't you check out the house before we unload any of our stuff."

Horace disappeared inside the abandoned house. The rest of the family waited. Only a few seconds passed when he came running out shouting, "Dad! He's right about those snakes! There's the biggest rattler I ever saw coiled up in there!" Grandpa followed Horace back inside. It was a very long five minutes before they returned with a headless six-foot rattler in hand.

In June of 1933, my mother's family got as far as the Estancia Valley in New Mexico in search of work. They were broke with only a loaf of bread left to feed a family of eight. They stopped at a farm owned by John

Casebolt to inquire about work. When he saw the old truck loaded with all their belongings and six hungry dirty kids, he said, "Yeah, my beans need workin' and looks like most'a those kids are big enough to grab a hoe handle." Grandpa thanked John when he brought food to their campsite that night. The next morning at sunrise, Jack and Bertie and their six kids were all at work in those bean fields.

By noon the blisters on their bare hands had broken and turned raw and bloody. They wrapped their hands in strips of rags and continued hoeing until sundown. The next day John Casebolt advanced them enough money to buy groceries and gloves. On Sunday, their day off, they moved into an old empty house outside town.

The Spanish name Estancia means Estate. The natural springs that existed in Estancia were the reason for farmers and ranchers to settle there. At that time dry land farms were still producing abundant beans in the area and Estancia was considered the "bean capital" of the state. Large storage buildings for beans stood next to the railroad tracks. Nearby were holding pens for cattle destined for shipment on the railroad.

State Highway 41 runs north and south; even today it is the main street of Estancia. Most of the businesses have long since closed. In 1933, however, Main Street ran for about two blocks, and the businesses included a drug store, café, feed store, hotel, dry goods store, the Busy Bee Saloon, and a grocery store.

The Torrance County Court House sat a block off the main street. The town park had a cement pond that was fed by a natural spring. There were two schools, a baseball park, and a rodeo grounds. At one time Estancia had a hand-operated printing press.

Most of the nine hundred residents lived on the west side of Highway 41 and the railroad tracks. This small number of people supported four churches: Methodist, Church of Christ, Catholic, and Baptist. There was plenty of religion to go around.

It was noted by the members of these houses of worship that the Counts family was in no hurry to join any of their groups. It was also noted that although the Counts were hard working people, they were very poor. Besides they were "newcomers." It was not that the family did not believe in God, for both Grandma and Grandpa had been brought up as fundamentalist Christian, but having perceived contempt by some people during their exodus from Oklahoma for their impoverished condition, the family was not anxious to subject themselves to criticism of the "solid citizens" of Estancia. Instead, they opted to work hard and mind their own business.

My mother's low opinion of religious hypocrites and mistrust of men was further influenced at an early age by a life-altering experience. Had I known her story when I was a child, I would not have wondered why she was so mistrustful of men and churchgoers. I would also have understood her defensive attitude where she and her children were concerned.

Bee had just turned fifteen the following summer and was again working in the bean fields. Although she did not think she was pretty, others did. Baggy work clothes might hide her blossoming figure, but nothing could deny the beauty of her face and lovely smile. She was not prepared for the attention her looks would attract, and she knew little or nothing about sex. In her family, sex was not something "good girls" discussed.

She was flattered when Dewy Blancett, the twenty-five-year-old son of a preacher, started noticing her. Dewy was working in the fields hauling beans to the storage buildings in town. He planned to follow in his father's footsteps to one day become a preacher. He had perfect manners, he didn't swear and he had a future ahead of him. In short, he was good husband material.

The first time she saw Dewey, Bee was standing at the end of the row of beans, wiping her forehead with a handkerchief. As he drove past and glanced her way, his mouth opened. About fifteen feet down the road he slammed on the brakes, put the truck in reverse, and backed up.

"You better start wearin' a hat to protect that pretty face," he said as he looked more closely. He seemed even more astonished when she smiled, showing perfectly white straight teeth.

"I know," Bee said shyly, "I just forgot it this morning." She was embarrassed and surprised that anyone would notice her, much less pay her a compliment. As he drove off she was flushed with pleasure as she continued hoeing in the hot sun. That was not the last time Dewey would make an excuse to talk to Bee.

At fifteen, Bee was not allowed to date. Her parents would certainly not have approved of her seeing a man in his twenties. This did not prevent her from being attracted to this charming man with his sparkling green eyes, curly brown hair and easy smile. She found herself looking forward to being near him more and more as they worked in the fields. The hard work and hot sun in the fields was made more tolerable at the thought of seeing Dewey.

As she began to fall in love with him and their romance blossomed, they found ways to meet in secret. It was not difficult in these stolen moments for Bee to be seduced by this handsome older man.

Her parents knew nothing of the affair until, during a hospital stay for an emergency appendectomy; the doctor came into the room and asked without fanfare, "Did you know that Beatrice is pregnant?"

Bee was as stunned as her parents. In her ignorance of matters sexual, she had no idea she was with child. Grandma put her hands over her face and started crying. Grandpa's voice was shaking when he finally spoke. "Sister Girl, tell us how this happened and who is responsible." Bee felt ashamed as she haltingly confessed to her affair with Dewey.

After her mother finally stopped crying and wringing her hands she turned to Bee and shook her head. "Well Beatrice, if you don't get married you'll just have to go to that home for unwed mothers in Albuquerque." Her voice cracked as she said, "This is a disgrace."

"Oh no, she won't, Bertie," Grandpa cut in. "She'll stay right here with us," he said as he patted his daughter's hand. "My girl ain't bad and we're gonna see her through this."

Grandpa's support at this critical point in her life might explain my mother's dedication to him when he grew old and sick and had no place to go. Grandma's condemnation would cause an unspoken rift that would last a lifetime.

Dewy's father, the preacher, held great sway over his son as did his mother. Dewey was dedicated to his parents and did not wish to disappoint them. When they learned of Bee's condition, his father forbade him to marry her. Whether their opposition to the marriage was because my mother's family did not attend their church or the fact that they were poor was never made clear. Whatever the reason, the results were devastating for my mother. She felt betrayed by the man she had innocently trusted. In spite of their professed beliefs, Dewy and his parents showed no intention to do the right thing by her. He ignored her for the most part until three years later when he asked to see the child she bore. By that time it was too little too late and she sent him on his way. Never to be a part of the baby's life.

She came to believe, for the most part, that many people attend church just for show. Her own situation was proof of that. At fifteen she had to face her situation alone and with a broken heart. She was robbed of her innocence and the man she loved. Her strength grew as did her resentment and distrust for men and "church people" in general.

She became a mother at fifteen and gave birth in her parent's home. Only her mother, who had resigned herself to the birth, and Dr. Wiggins were there. Because of her young age and unmarried status at the birth of my older brother, Willie, Dr. Wiggins begged her to let him have her beautiful baby boy to raise as his own. What he didn't realize was that Mama would never give up any of her children under any circumstance. She felt it was her duty and responsibility to raise and protect them; to do less would be nothing short of an unforgivable sin.

"No, doctor, I could never abandon this baby," she said as she caressed Willie's small head. "He's mine to take care of." In a soft but firm voice she continued, "I'm not a shiftless no-good, I just made a mistake."

Mama fell in love with Willie at first sight. He would always be her special child. He was a beautiful baby who turned into a handsome youngster with wavy hair and green eyes. Everyone in Mama's family loved Willie, especially Grandma. Once she held him in her arms, she was just as much in love with him as Mama. As he grew older his easy going nature, generosity and sense of humor made those around him adore him completely.

Mama rarely went anywhere after Willie was born; but when he was about a year old, she went to a rodeo in Estancia along with members of her family. Of course, she took Willie with her. She had turned sixteen and though simply dressed, was pretty enough to attract the attention of Lee Hollan Tracy, who was then only nineteen years old. He was a contestant in the rodeo, tall and handsome with black wavy hair and brown eyes.

Much to Mama's surprise when Hollan started to the chutes to mount his horse, he walked to the bleachers where she was sitting and tossed her his hat. When she caught it, he winked and smiled. "Ma'am, would you hold on to this while I bust this bronc out?"

Mama, flushed with pleasure, sat speechless.

After finishing his ride he returned for his hat. "I'm Hollan Tracy, and I've noticed you around. What's your name?"

Mama smiled at him, blushing slightly. "I'm Bee," she said quietly, "and that baby settin' on his Grandma's lap is my boy, Willie."

This did not ruffle Hollan one bit. He just smiled and said, "Well, I'd like to get to know you both better."

Hollan Tracy, Bertie's father, about 26 years old

Chapter Three

The attraction was mutual and Bee was especially drawn to Hollan's tough direct approach. She admired a man who could stand up for himself and she would later boast of his fighting prowess. Her heart was not entirely mended from her first romantic encounter and her innocent trust had been permanently replaced with a wariness of men. Hollan's acceptance of Willie and the fact he refused to judge Bee's past was of utmost importance to her. After a brief courtship, she accepted his proposal of marriage.

Hollan was not a bully but he did enjoy participating in local prize fights and he had a reputation as "the one to beat." Word came one day that somebody in Estancia wanted to challenge him to a fight.

"Hollan," Bee said, when he walked in from work, "your dad came by to say there was a man down at the Busy Bee waitin' to fight you."

"Well," Hollan shrugged, "soon as I eat some supper, we'll go down and see what it's all about."

After their dinner of beans and cornbread, Hollan and Bee went into town. They found the challenger, a man in his early twenties, sitting at the saloon bar, his hands taped and ready for a bout. Hollan tried to discourage him.

"Why don't we just have a beer instead?"

The young man nodded toward an older fellow sitting beside him. "No, my dad thinks I can whip you. Besides he has a lot of money ridin' on this fight."

The old man nodded in agreement. "Yeah, we traveled over two hundred miles to see if what we heard about you is true."

It was obvious who had covered one of the bets as Hollan's dad, Jack Tracy, sat at the other end of the bar squinting over a Pabst Blue Ribbon.

Seeing there was no way to talk the man out of fighting, Hollan punched him with his deadly left hook, and sent him flying backwards across the floor.

"Out cold as a wedge," one observer noted.

When the young man came to he struggled to his feet and on wobbly legs shuffled toward the bar. "They sure as hell weren't kidding, Tracy," he said as he rubbed his jaw. "You are one tough son of a bitch. I'll have that beer now."

Bee was proud of Hollan and she loved the excitement of the fight. She described it many times. It was as close as she ever came to bragging on him. This event may have been the beginning of her propensity to settle matters with her fists instead of with words.

My parents had been married about a year and Bee was eighteen and due with their first child. At that time Daddy made a living as a ranch hand breaking horses for Jim Albritton, a rancher, whose wife Thelma Ruth, became fast friends with Mama. Mama and Daddy lived in a small house on Jim's ranch, which made it convenient for Thelma to stop by and visit.

That July 17, 1937, Jessie was born prematurely. It was a difficult birth followed by bad news from Dr. Wiggins. "Bee," he said sadly, "I'm afraid this baby probably won't make it." He shook his head as he held Jessie in one hand emphasizing his tiny size.

Grandma Counts, who had assisted Dr. Wiggins with the delivery, hesitantly agreed. "Beatrice, he might be right. Just look how fragile this little thing is. Why, even his skin looks raw."

"Just tell me what I need to do to help him stay alive." Bee pleaded tearfully, "I'll do anything, just tell me."

Before he left, Dr. Wiggins told Bee how to care for Jessie but also warned her not to get her hopes up, that the odds were against him. He told her to keep Jessie very warm, which was no problem because it was the middle of a very hot July. He told her not to allow sick people near him, which also was not a problem as they were so isolated and rarely had company. He told her to keep everything around him very clean, which she would do even without having been told. Grandma could stay only a few days. This left Mama alone to care for Jessie and Willie, who was now a two year old toddler. Daddy had to work long hours and could offer little help.

Those first weeks were torture for her. She spent many sleepless nights following the doctor's instructions. She watched Jessie constantly. He was so tiny she had to place him on a pillow to hold him while he nursed. The times he seemed to stop breathing she would pat his back and rub his tiny feet until his breathing became regular again.

Because he was premature, Jessie developed a heart condition that lasted the first few years of his life. He also had poor hearing. But in spite of all this, the tiny bald wrinkled Jessie grew into a cute little blond-haired boy with pale blue eyes. Hollan loved Willie, but he was very partial to Jessie. Willie was not bothered by this and seemed to understand that Jessie needed extra love and care.

Mama loved Daddy and considered herself an equal partner in their relationship. She didn't hesitate when he asked her to help move a herd of horses from Moriarty to Estancia in the dead of winter. She left Willie and Jessie with Grandma and saddled up to help Hollan and her brother Dick, herd the horses. Unfortunately, a winter storm rolled slowly into the valley, turning into a blizzard. After hours of struggling through the blowing snow, the horses began to slow to a near stop. Knowing they had to press onward or freeze, Hollan and Dick dismounted and led the horses on foot. It was getting dark and just when they thought they would not survive the storm, the wind died down just enough for them to see a flicker of light in the distance. They forged onward. The light turned out to be a lamp in the window of a ranch house. The rancher let them pen the horses in his corral. Bee was too cold to dismount so Hollan had to lift her out of the saddle and carry her into the welcomed warmth of the ranch house. The blizzard lasted through the night leaving mountainous snowdrifts in its wake. It took three days before people were able to get through the snow drifts. While digging out, they found two people frozen to death. One was a man who had gotten lost after leaving his stranded car and another was a sheepherder who died along with some of his heard only about two-hundred yards from shelter. In spite of knowing they could have frozen to death, Bee did not blame Hollan for putting her in danger. She would follow him anywhere, and liked showing she could be as tough as any man.

House where Bertie was born

In the summer of 1939 my folks moved from the ranch to a house on the outskirts of Estancia. Their new home had two small rooms, no electricity, and no indoor plumbing. There was even a chicken coop on the property where Mama planned to raise chickens. But first she had to shoot and kill a coyote that was living under an old abandoned car hood so it wouldn't eat the eggs and kill the chickens. Using Hollan's 30-30 rifle, mama stuck the barrel under the car hood and blasted that coyote.

The exterior of this house was badly weathered. Inside, the walls were covered with old wallpaper stamped with a floral pattern that had long since faded into the gray background. But as usual, Mama cleaned it up, kept it that way, and generally made it feel like home.

She was glad to live closer to town because any day she would give birth to her third child. At least this time it would be a full term baby. At 2:30 in the morning, when labor began, she was grateful that Daddy was by her side and not at work.

She touched his shoulder, "Wake up, Hollan, I believe it's time. Go get my mama and the doctor."

My brothers were still groggy with sleep when Daddy loaded them into the old car to take them to their grandparent's house. There Mama's younger sister, Virginia, would care for them while I made my entrance into the world.

Willie and Jessie enjoyed their brief stay at Grandma's house. Virginia kept frail, two-year-old Jessie inside, while Willie and Mama's baby brother, Murrel, both four, were allowed to play outside. They spent most of that day on the bed of an old flatbed truck, playing games and trying out some cuss words they had previously overheard.

They were laughing and rolling out the words like a foreign language when Virginia approached on their blind side.

"What do you youngin's think you're doin'?" she demanded.

"We're talkin' Mexican," Murrel responded proudly. Virginia thought otherwise and scolded them with the threat of a spankin'.

That same afternoon on October 30, 1939, I arrived after twelve hours of hard labor. To my mother's relief, a smiling Dr. Wiggins said, "Bee, you have a healthy nine-pound girl."

Grandma Counts immediately laid claim to me. "Oh, Beachie," she purred, using her pet name for Mama. "Can we please name her "Bertie" . . . for me?"

For months before my birth, Grandma had campaigned for a namesake.

She strongly discouraged Mama from naming me after her best friend, Thelma Ruth, saying through tight lips, "Beatrice, that woman is nothin' but a strumpet. I don't know why you think so much of her."

When Bee remained loyal to Thelma Ruth, Grandma harshly elaborated, "She's a cheat and a woman of easy virtue. Anybody can see she knows her way around men. You mark my word, one of these days she's gonna show you what stripe a dog she is." That was Grandma's way of inferring that Thelma was a no good scoundrel.

Mama had already decided the path of least resistance was to grant Grandma's wish, and she gave her the gift she would always treasure; a namesake: Bertie Ruth.

Not surprisingly I was Grandma's favorite grandchild. Grandpa Counts, however, was not impressed that Grandma had a namesake. He had wanted my brother Jessie to be named "Andrew Jackson" after him but had been ignored. When Grandma returned home and proudly announced, "Well, Jackson, they named the baby girl Bertie," Grandpa sharply responded, "I don't care if they named her Chicken Shit. They haven't named anyone after me yet."

In spite of his first colorful reaction, he seemed to adore me, never once referring to me as Chicken Shit.

Bertie Counts, Bertie's grandmother and namesake

Chapter Four

My parent's marriage was a happy one and from all accounts was passionate as well. They enjoyed going to dances and Bee was proud to be on the arm of a handsome, man whose presence demanded respect and admiration. They made a fine couple; she with her blond hair done up nicely and her pretty face with just a touch of makeup to emphasize her turquoise eyes; he with his black wavy hair, sparkling brown eyes, and cowboy tan set off against the white shirt he always wore to dances.

At one particular dance, Mama's best friend, Thelma Ruth confided that Mama should "keep her eye on that good looking husband." She had no idea Thelma's advice was a thinly veiled threat of her intentions.

I was about a year old when Daddy began trapping coyotes and other livestock predators. Ranchers paid a bounty for these animals, and Daddy sold coyote and bobcat pelts from the animals he trapped. His work forced us to move to southern New Mexico between Las Cruces and El Paso, Texas where there was a demand for his pelts. No housing was available in the area, so for that summer we camped in a tent by the Rio Grande River.

The prairie and desert areas of New Mexico, with their wide-open spaces and mountains appearing timidly in the distance, have always left me feeling lonesome. Mama must have felt the same, but had little time to dwell on such thoughts. She was busy "keeping house" in a tent with three children, ages one, three, and five. Fortunately we only lived in the tent for about four months.

We would sometimes drive several miles over dusty, rutted roads to a little place called Ore Grande to pick up a few supplies. Daddy would retire to the bar for a beer or two while Mama sipped soft drinks with us kids. At that time she didn't drink anything stronger than soda pop.

She was determined to be a good wife and mother and did so without complaint. I believe she enjoyed those times when we all accompanied Hollan to attend his trap lines.

We had no telephone or any other form of communication while living in the trapping camps. It was Daddy's grandpa Allen who traveled from Estancia to bring the news that Hollan had been offered a Government Trapping job. This was good news. We were struggling just to get by. A low paying government job with regular pay checks was preferable to the irregular income from selling hides and collecting bounties.

"I'm glad I got the job, Bee," Daddy said, hugging her. "They'll even give me a government vehicle to run trap lines."

"I'm glad, too, Hollan, I just hope we can find a better place to live."

He did, too. Tent life had been hard on his family, especially his wife.

The government job would require frequent moves. Only a certain number of animals could be removed from one designated area before Daddy would be required to reset his traps in another. His first assignment for the government was trapping on the Malcolm McGregory bombing range where the rancher who owned the property ran cows and sheep and wanted it rid of predators that killed his livestock.

The United States was about to become involved in World War II and this range land was also used for bombing practice. Planes would drop their small bombs filled with sand, and later, the debris would be hauled away in trucks.

It was fall when we moved into an old ranch house that had several rooms, some of which had been boarded up and used as storage. The house sat on the edge of the Malcolm McGregory property miles from any town or neighbors, and although the airplanes could be seen heading for their practice targets, our house was not near the areas where they dropped their bombs. Mama didn't seem to mind the isolation as long as she had her children and a husband who came home every night.

On a rare trip back to Estancia, we stopped by to see Grandma and Grandpa Counts. Mama was especially fond of her younger brother, Murrel. He was Grandma's last child and because she had little breast milk to feed him he was poorly nourished and cranky. He was born two months before Willie and Mama helped care for him. When he cried she would sing to him as she carried him around. After Willie was born Mama had an abundance of milk and breastfed him along with Willie for the next few months. This created a bond between the two boys and at five years old they were still close. Murrel even gave Willie his small dog as a token of his adoration.

Being the baby of the family, Murrel was spoiled. As we started to leave, he started crying, "Mama, let me go home with Willie."

"No," Grandma patiently explained, "you can't go home with them Murrel. It's too far away."

"I'll just kill myself if I can't go," Murrel screamed as tears made tracks down his dirty face. With that hysterical declaration, he started running into bushes and brush and rolling on the ground. He emerged from his tantrum with only minor bruises and abrasions, a snotty nose and red eyes. His fit throwing didn't work and he continued to sob as we drove away without him. We only took his gift to Willie, the little dog named Brownie.

"Come here, little honey," Willie whispered as he held Brownie to his chest, "I'll take you everyplace I go." They fell asleep in the back seat as we traveled home.

Our water came from a windmill that pumped into an old wooden tank on a tall platform. Willie, noticing several wooden pegs in the sides of the tank asked, "What made all those holes in the tank, Daddy?"

"They say its where some outlaw horse thieves had a shoot-out with the law," Daddy answered.

Willie was impressed with the story of the shoot-out and the many bullet holes remaining as testament. His young imagination worked overtime as he excitedly reported to Mama. "One of those outlaws was shot twenty times before he fell off on his head."

Although we lived in a desolate snake-infested area, Willie loved to play outside, examining every bug, sand turtle, or worm he could find in that desert. Jessie and I watched him one day catch a small sand turtle. At first the turtle would retract its feet and head into its shell. But finally it got used to Willie's stroking and walked around, head out. Willie was delighted with this development.

"Look," he said excitedly, "I think I can get him to plow a field for me." He held the front of the turtle up while allowing its little back feet to drag in the sand creating small furrows in the sand. The turtle finally lost patience with Willie and bit his finger. Willie yelped and stuck his finger in his mouth.

"I guess you don't want to make rows after all," he said softly to the turtle as he set him on the ground to return to his home in the desert.

Willie's little dog, Brownie, always led the way on their outside adventures and barked loudly if ever they encountered danger. Brownie was a brave little soul who had a bite as well as a bark. He once killed a big bull snake by shaking and biting it to death. When Daddy was tracking a bobcat with his big hounds, Brownie got loose and ran with the hounds to attack the cat. With his sharp claws, the bobcat grabbed the small dog by the top of the head before flinging him away. Poor little Brownie wound up with a swollen head and eyes completely closed.

Jessie, who adored his older brother, Willie, usually tagged along on these exploratory missions. Fortunately, Jessie was napping the day Willie and Brownie decided to venture into the desert beyond the old ranch house. As they made their way around mesquite bushes and cactus in the hot sand,

Brownie suddenly stopped. His little body trembled but he stood his ground, stiffly blocking Willie from going ahead.

Then Brownie began to bark. "What's the matter, little honey?" Willie asked.

At that moment Willie saw a huge rattlesnake coiled and ready to strike, its rattles deafening in the afternoon heat.

Willie was well aware of the danger. It took him only a few moments before he turned and raced through the bushes back to the house. "Mama," he cried. "Come look at the big snake little honey's barking at!"

The shouting aroused Jessie from his nap, and he in turn, woke me as he slid off the bed. My brother had no intention of missing all the excitement.

"No, Jessie, you stay here with Bertie," Mama said sharply. But by the time she got Jessie and me settled down it was too late for Brownie; Mama found Willie's little dog fallen on the back step, dying from the rattlesnake's venomous bite. Sobbing in anguish, Willie cradled Brownie in his arms. He rocked back and forth, whispering, "little honey, please don't die, please don't die, I love you too much."

Mama cried too, but her tears were mostly because she could not absorb Willie's pain. As Mama dug a grave for Brownie, she could not stop thinking what if Willie had been bitten. She would not have gotten help in time for her oldest child and that thought was unbearable. She felt Brownie had saved Willie's life.

Jessie loved Daddy more than he loved anyone. He always cried to go along when Daddy went to attend to his trap lines. Sometimes, if the trip was short enough, Daddy would take him. More often, Jessie had to stay home.

One day, Jessie was particularly desperate to accompany our father. "You can't go today, Jess," Daddy said. "I'll be gone too long."

Jessie was still crying as Daddy carried his gear to the old panel wagon. "Let me go with you, Daddy, please let me go with you," Jessie whined. He hovered near the wagon while Daddy said his goodbyes. Mama held me into the car window for one last kiss. As Daddy started to back away from the house, Jessie broke free from Mama's hand and darted behind the wagon.

"Stop, Daddy! Stop!" Willie shrieked. The bumper knocked Jessie to the ground and the back wheel ran over him.

"My God!" Daddy jumped from the wagon and dragged Jessie free. Daddy's tan face drained white as he carried his son into the house.

"Let me have him, he's not breathing," Mama screamed.

But Jessie's ashen face and blue lips were deceiving. Amazingly, he'd only had the breath knocked out of him. After what seemed like forever, he started squalling with increasing intensity. The ground had been softened by a recent rain and Jessie was only bruised. This accident didn't dampen his desire to be with his Daddy—a desire that would later cause him untold grief.

Bee, Bertie's mother, about 23 years old, married to Hollan Tracy

Chapter Five

After trapping on the bombing range, Daddy's next assignment was near Pinon, New Mexico, a dot on the map midway between Alamogordo and Artesia. There we shared a house that was partitioned off to provide two living quarters. Willie's first grade teacher lived in one side.

Pinon was named for the trees that cover the area hillsides. Mama could not have imagined at that time that many years later one of those lovely peaceful hillsides would become her final resting place.

Not long after our move, Daddy made a quick trip back to Estancia on a job-related matter. With Willie now in school we couldn't go along. We all missed Daddy and in anticipation of his return home, Mama washed her hair and put on lipstick. When he walked through the door he was greeted with hugs and kisses from us kids; Mama waited for her turn until last.

"Did you see Jim and Thelma Ruth?" Mama inquired. There was no telephone in the area and she was hoping for news from her best friend.

"Yeah, just for a little while," Hollan shrugged. "They said to tell you hello." He quickly changed the subject as Daddy then gave Jessie an extra hug and handed Willie a brown paper sack. "Here is some candy I brought for you kids. Don't eat it all before supper."

Although Mama was disappointed, she didn't think it peculiar that Hollan had so little to say about the encounter with their friends. He had his moods and was not a big talker in general.

As usual, Daddy left early the next morning to check his traps while Mama attended to seemingly endless domestic chores. She was sorting laundry, looking for clothes to be washed when she undid his bedroll.

Mama was stunned at what she saw; silky red pajamas. Another woman's pajamas! The very pajamas Mama had once admired when Thelma Ruth was showing off her purchases after a shopping trip to Albuquerque!

Mama began shaking and felt sick to her stomach. She sank down onto the edge of the bed. This was a direct message from Thelma Ruth, a message that could not have been clearer had it been painted across the sky in big red letters—she wanted Mama to know that her husband was unfaithful.

Mama could not hold back the tears. This betrayal of her best friend and her husband was cruel and unthinkable. She had barely gotten over the heartache of her first love . . . and now this.

Jessie and I knew there was trouble but couldn't imagine what it was. When Willie came home from school we ran to meet him. "Somethin's wrong with Mama," Jessie said. "She's just been layin' on the bed all day."

We marched behind Willie through the house and to Mama's bedside. Sure enough, she was huddled on the mattress, her face turned to the wall. "Mama?" Willie finally whispered, "What's wrong? Are you sick?"

Mama sighed. For a minute nothing happened. Then she drew Willie to her, swung her legs over the side of the bed, and said without much conviction, "Nothin's wrong, honey. I'm fine. Everything is going to be all right."

We weren't so sure.

When Daddy came home that evening Mama was waiting at the door and my brothers and I were watching from the kitchen. He no sooner stepped inside when Mama thrust out her hand with Thelma Ruth's bright red pajamas. "Do you know anything about these?"

Daddy opened his mouth and shut it again. He just shook his head.

"I found them in your bedroll," Mama said. Her voice was low and steely.

Daddy shook his head again. "I don't have any idea how they got there," he said.

Even as young as we were, we kids knew he'd made some kind of mistake. And then he dug himself in deeper because he kept on denying. "I just bedded down in their bunkhouse, Bee, that's all."

But the guilt in his eyes spoke louder than the lie on his tongue.

"It's bad enough that you did it," Mama said. "It's even worse that you lie about it."

Daddy held out his hands, palms up. "I'm sorry, Bee, but she's been after me a long time. Listen to me, hon, I swear it won't happen again."

My brothers and I had no idea what they were talking about or why Mama was so upset about a pair of red pajamas. We figured Thelma Ruth had some more and wouldn't miss that pair too much.

More words of contrition followed that night and for days after, but the trust was broken. With three kids to consider, Mama decided to make the best of it. She would try to hold the marriage together. But their relationship was seriously damaged and the distance only grew between them.

We could not understand why our Mama and Daddy stopped being happy and didn't hug much anymore.

Years later when recalling the story of Thelma's pajamas in Daddy's bedroll, it struck me odd that her anger wasn't directed toward Thelma, instead of Daddy. I asked, "Mama, why were you so mad at Daddy and not Thelma Ruth?"

Mama sharply replied, "Thelma never made me any promises; your daddy did!"

From Pinon we moved to the small hamlet of Hope, which is 27 miles west of Artesia. The only positive thing about the place was its name. The few trees in the area were scraggly and shadeless. They struggled from the earth just inches from the perimeters of dilapidated buildings, seeking some sanctuary from the harshness of the prairie.

There was an earthen tank not far from our house in Hope where Willie loved to try to catch fish. It mattered little that the only fish in the tank were small, ugly catfish unfit to eat; the *challenge* to catch them was what mattered to Willie. Like tiny disciples, Jessie and I followed him everywhere he went.

I was standing beside him one warm afternoon as he prepared to cast his line into the murky water. "Stand outta the way, Bertie, I'm gonna catch me a golly whopper!" he shouted, thrusting back the pole.

I had just bent over to retrieve a marble when the fish hook snagged my panty-clad rear end. It scratched and stung and I began squalling at the top of my lungs, "I hurt! I hurt!"

For several agonizing minutes, Willie tried to free the hook from my drawers. In the end, my stamping and screeching made his task impossible. We lurched back to the house with me firmly attached to the end of his fishing line. I can't recall what action Mama took, but my lack of desire to ever fish again was probably influenced by that incident.

Our parent's relationship continued to deteriorate, going from bad to worse and for us kids from sad to sadder. They did not argue all the time, but there was an air of hostility between them that made family life uneasy.

In the summer of 1942, we moved from Hope to Sixteen Springs for a brief time and then to Weed, a tiny village in the Sacramento Mountains. The nearest town of any consequence was, and still is, Alamogordo.

Back then there were only three homes in Weed with inside plumbing and electricity. The schools had electricity but it would be eight years before indoor plumbing was installed.

My grandpa and grandma Counts, along with Mama's brothers, Bill and Murrel, moved to Weed about the same time we did. World War II had started and Mama's brother, Dick, had been drafted into the Army. Times were tough and everyone had to work hard to make a living. Bill went to work on the Circle Cross Ranch as a cowboy. Mama's parents and Murrel lived in Blue Water Canyon. There Grandpa decided to go into hog farming using some of the money Dick had sent home from the Army. The decision to use the money to raise hogs was made without Dick's knowledge or approval. When Dick came home on furlough from the Army he wasn't very happy about owning hogs and told Grandpa in no uncertain terms, "Get rid of those hogs, Dad, I ain't cut out to be no hog farmer." Grandpa sold what hogs he could and butchered the rest. This was a good thing as far as Willie and Murrel were concerned because numerous times they had to herd the hogs out of the neighbors Lloyd and Mabel Burgess's cornfield. An old sow was the main culprit in breaking out of the pigpen to invade the cornfield.

"I think that old sow can climb straight up a wall," Willie told Grandpa. "There ain't no pen gonna hold her in."

Having her family close was a comfort to Mama as her marriage was failing. To us kids, having our relatives around was fun. Willie and Jessie played with Murrel and Grandma and my uncles doted over me.

When Uncle Dick was discharged from the Army, he rode the bus back to Estancia where he had left the nineteen horses he owned. His favorite was a big bay named Rusty that he had broken as a colt. With Rusty as his mount he moved his herd of horses to Weed. He started with nineteen in Estancia and arrived in Weed with twenty-one. How he came by the extras is anybody's guess. He drove the herd through the Malpais and into the Sacramento Mountains. The trip was over two hundred miles and he stopped only for the horses to drink and graze. He arrived in Weed and rented pasture land. He had not been in Weed many days when he decided to ride his beloved horse, Rusty, up the canyon to the Village of Sacramento. This was the last time Dick was to ride Rusty. Two miles out of Weed, Rusty fell to his knees and died. Dick was so broken hearted that he auctioned off the rest of his horses and never owned more than one or two horses the rest of his life.

My grandparents and uncles lived in the Weed area for a couple of years, then for a time in Cox Canyon, near Cloudcroft. Next they moved to Sixteen Springs to work in a sawmill. While they were living at the sawmill there was a dispute between two neighbors over a wooden barrel used to catch the rainwater draining from the roof of the house. The argument became so heated that one man shot and killed the other. This incident illustrated how important water was to New Mexicans. Without access to cistern water, drinking water had to be hauled in barrels. This meant long trips to natural springs, creeks or wells. Runoff rainwater was valued.

In 1944 my grandparents left Sixteen Springs and moved to Taos, New Mexico for a year or two and then on to Albuquerque.

Although I was only four years old, the reason I remember so clearly the day I talked Jessie into wading into the flooding ravine, was because the following day our big heartbreak came calling. Daddy came home from a long absence on one of his trapping jobs and my parents' marital problems came to a head.

The memory that stands out most regarding my folks' marriage was the final showdown that ended it. I cannot recall their actual words, just bits and pieces of a loud argument that ended when Daddy walked out the door. We were all crying, with Jessie crying the hardest.

"Daddy, don't go! Daddy, don't go!" he screamed as he clung to his pants leg.

I ran to Mama and hugged her leg. "Mama, I don't want Daddy to leave us. Why is he goin'?"

Mama picked me up and hugged me to her breast. "Hush now," her voice cracked, "we're gonna be all right. You'll see Daddy again."

Daddy gently removed Jessie's clinging hands from his pants and with tears streaming down his own face, walked out the door. As the door closed, Jessie collapsed to the floor, his shoulders heaved with sobs. His grief was palpable.

I felt so sad and empty, partly because Daddy was leaving but mostly because Jessie was so devastated and heartbroken. This empty feeling of heartbreak would be a binding tie for the rest of our lives.

Although life had been tough to that point, we had no idea that the hardships would grow worse throughout our childhood.

Weed, New Mexico as it appeared in 1942

Chapter Six

After our parents' showdown in Weed and their marriage ended, my brothers and I stayed with Daddy infrequently. As a government trapper, he moved around a lot so we couldn't visit him as often as we would have liked. He was also working in some isolated places, in camps that were not fit for young children.

The first time we stayed with Daddy after the divorce he came to Weed and took Jessie and me to Ora Grande where he was trapping during the day and tending bar at night. Willie opted to stay with Mama that particular time.

Daddy took us with him to check his trap lines and then kept an eye on us while he tended bar. He was living in a room in the back of the bar and that's where we slept.

One night he scolded me for drinking the rest of a Coke from a bottle left by a customer. Daddy rarely scolded me and I was hurt and mad at him. When he put me to bed in the backroom that night, and after I had cried myself into dry hiccups, I decided to make him think I had run away. After Jessie went to sleep, I slipped out of bed and crawled beneath it—as far as I dared to in the dark.

As tears streamed from my eyes into my ears where they demanded the attention of my fingertips, I thought of how I missed my mama, which brought forth even more tears. Before crying myself to sleep on the cool floor, my last thoughts were, "Daddy, you're gonna be so sad when you can't find your little girl." Unfortunately I wasn't awake to see if he was sad or not when he came in, scooped me up, and put me in bed to finish the night on a soft mattress.

The following day I was wearing a ring with a little red stone that someone had given me. The stone was cut glass, I am sure, but I treasured that ring. I was playing outside in the sand, poking a stick at what I later learned was a scorpion. Suddenly, the stick broke and the scorpion wrapped itself around my little finger. In terror, I started slinging my hand to get rid of it and the ring, along with the scorpion, flew off my finger. Although I was not stung, I ran to Daddy, crying and screaming, "A worm got on my finger and took my ring." The tears flowed as we searched among the tumbleweeds and red ant mounds for my ring. We never found it. My sorrow at losing my ring reminded me of my bigger loss; my mother wasn't here. So that brought on more tears.

My daddy must have felt overwhelmed trying to care for two children, four and six, because shortly after that he took us back home to Mama. I was so glad to see her. She hugged and kissed me as though I had been gone for years instead of weeks. Jessie was glad to be back with Mama, too, but in a couple days he started crying for Daddy. He seemed to miss Daddy more than any one of us and never accepted his absence. I tried to comfort Jessie. I missed Daddy too.

When I was five years old Jessie and I were with Daddy for about a month. We stayed with him in the house in Estancia where I was born. As we dug through boxes of old musty possessions I was comforted to find things that belonged to us when we were a family.

I spent some time that summer playing with the neighboring kids who lived across the road. Their last name was Shirley. The family had a mean hunting hound that had to be tied up because it would bite anything that moved. It belonged to an uncle, Austin Shirley, who seemed to have an equally bad disposition. Years later I would learn that part of his peculiarity was the result of his experience as a World War II soldier. He was a survivor of the Batan Death March. But at the time I thought his temperament was influenced by an incident I overheard Daddy and Mary Shirley discussing.

"What's wrong with Austin," Daddy inquired. "He seems out of sorts lately."

"Well, you know he's not been the same since him and Donald came back from trapping camp the other day. While they were out there, Austin came down with the mumps and when the swellin' went down on him, he got real sick. His private parts were causing him a lot of pain and it didn't help none for Donald to accidently doctor him with horse liniment instead of the rubbin' alcohol. Guess it was dark in camp and Donald couldn't make out the difference in the bottles. Austin ain't talked much to anybody since."

Whatever the cause, we kept a respectful distance from both Austin and his dog when walking to the earth tank behind their corrals. Both this tank and the metal stock tank gave off the mossy odor of water, a smell I loved as it promised life in the dry prairie.

One summer day I started across the dirt road to play with the Shirley kids. Suddenly, I was stopped by the rattling of an enormous rattlesnake coiled before me in the middle of the road. I stared hypnotized at that rattler whose forked tongue quickly flicked in and out. Our eyes locked for a few seconds. Then my brain kicked into gear, "Daddy! Daddy! Daddy!" I screamed. "A snake!"

Daddy came running with a shovel. "Just stay back, Bertie," he cautioned. He killed the snake, and then gathered me into his arms in a bear hug. I always liked it when Daddy, who was such a tall man, swept me up from the ground into his strong arms. I felt safe and liked the sound of his slow reassuring voice. Jessie also appreciated his size and strength. He once told me he felt the safest and happiest when he slept beside his Daddy.

After the rattlesnake scare I spent part of the afternoon with the Shirley clan watching baby chicks peck their way to freedom from eggs placed on the floor in sunlight. It always seemed a miracle how they changed from sticky wet little creatures into lovable balls of fluff on toothpick legs.

Mary Shirley was a generous woman who made us feel welcome. Her kitchen held delicious aromas: the yeasty smell of baked bread and the sweet scent of fresh milk stored for sale in metal cans out on the cooler porch. Whenever she decided to prepare homemade ice cream, Daddy furnished the ice and elbow grease. While he cranked the handle of the ice cream maker we hovered eagerly. Our reward: sweet creamy ice cream flavored with fresh fruit and vanilla.

Daddy was at a loss on handling kids, and we took full advantage of his inexperience by extorting bribes in exchange for good behavior. One Saturday night we hit the jackpot when Daddy wanted to go to a dance and leave us with Grandma Tracy. Recognizing an opportunity, I said sweetly, "Daddy, I've been lookin' at a teddy bear in the drugstore and boy, I would love to have it."

"Well maybe we can get it for you for stayin' here with your Grandma."

"If she gets a teddy bear, then I want a pocketknife." Jessie chimed in. "But I want it tonight."

The deal was brokered and Daddy agreed to go the drugstore right then to get our bribes. After giving us our booty but before he could make his departure, Jessie proceeded to renege on his part of the bargain. He tuned up and started crying.

"But Daddy I don't want the knife anymore," he squalled. "I want to go with you."

"No, Jessie, "I'm goin' to a dance, you can't go this time."

As Daddy went out the door Jessie threw his knife down and ran after him, screaming, "I wanna go! Let me go!"

I then witnessed an unusual event. Daddy spanked Jessie. After the butt warming, I retired to Grandma Tracy's bed with my ill-gotten gains and said not another word.

That summer, when Daddy was at work I would walk from our house, across vacant lots to Grandma Tracy's house. I would stay until he came home with Jessie, who usually went with him to check traps. In addition to trapping, Daddy was operating a bulldozer to earn extra money from ranchers building earth tanks. The one time he took me with him on an excavation job, I got sick on cantaloupe and Hershey bars. I also took my shoes off and cried when the sun-baked rocks burned the soles of my feet. Daddy had to climb down from the bulldozer to carry me to the shade of a cedar tree. The only thing I liked about the whole experience was sleeping under the stars that night and listening to Daddy tell us stories until we could no longer hold our eyes open.

I spent the rest of those summer days playing around Grandma's house and occasionally walking downtown to the drugstore for an ice cream cone. I liked to eat Grandma's homemade jam and bread as I sat in her front-porch swing.

I remember my grandpa Jack Tracy only because he seemed mysterious to me. With his gray hair, brown eyes, and weathered dark skin, he looked like an old Indian. He didn't talk much and occasionally tipped the bottle a bit more than Grandma approved of. One of the few times my brother Willie came with us to Estancia, Grandpa got out his old black Chevy and took Willie and Daddy's younger brother, Waylon, who was Willie's age, out driving. The headlights—mounted on top of the fenders—provided a handhold for the boys, who sat still as mastheads astride the headlights. Behind the steering wheel, Grandpa gave them a wild bone-bumping ride across that ocean of prairie. It didn't matter if they saw jackrabbits, coyotes, or sheep on those rides—the exhilaration of that fender-surfing proved excitement enough.

In west Texas in the fall of 1909, Grandpa Tracy married Grandma Allen, a large-boned soft-spoken woman. After the wedding they moved with her family to New Mexico. It was rumored that, as a young boy, Grandpa Jack Tracy had witnessed a hanging from a bridge by a group of men. The hanged man had allegedly murdered and robbed Grandma's uncle, a doctor, as he was returning from a house call. The vigilantes tracked the suspect to his home and extracted their own form of justice.

Upon their arrival in Estancia, New Mexico, Grandma's father and Grandpa Tracy became sheep ranchers. When Grandpa Allen passed away he left his ranch to Grandma Tracy. While Grandpa Tracy was running the sheep ranch, a local thief, by the name of Farnsworth, allegedly kept stealing sheep, and illegally letting his livestock graze and water on Grandpa's land. When Grandpa caught him stealing sheep he dragged him over to his side of the fence and shot him. At that time, stealing livestock was frowned upon by the law, and Grandpa received no jail time. No doubt witnessing the earlier vigilante lynching left an imprint on Grandpa Jack.

Grandma Tracy gave birth to nine children. Of those nine, there were two sets of twin girls. The first twin's lives ended in tragedy. In 1924, while living on the sheep ranch, Grandma rose early one morning to care for some orphaned lambs and left the five-year-old twins in the house. It was later determined that one of the little girl's gown caught fire as she was tending a wood stove. Grandma heard the screaming and rushed into the house where she smothered the flames but was unable to save her daughter's life. Grandma was still in mourning when they moved from the ranch into town, to a house built near the main highway. A year later, the surviving twin, was struck and killed by a truck in front of the house as Grandma watched in horror.

Even after suffering all that pain and grief Grandma remained a sweet happy person. The only time I heard of her losing her temper was when Grandpa Tracy, who had taken to drinking too much, came home on a bender. After stripping his clothes down to his long handled underwear he went into the kitchen in search of something to eat. He staggered into the kitchen stove and knocked off a large pan of jam that Grandma had left to cool before canning.

Grandpa lost his footing in the slick, sticky mess and slid to the floor. "Damnit, Ida Mae," he yelled. "What the hell is this stuff?"

Grandma found him wallowing around in the jam and gave him tit-for-tat. "Jack, you get yourself up from there and change those underwear."

It took him several tries, but he finally got up, staggered to the bedroom, and slid between Grandma's clean sheets in his sticky underwear. He promptly passed out.

The harder Grandma worked to clean the jam off the floor, the madder she got. Finally, she collected her sewing kit, tiptoed into the bedroom, and sewed the sheets together around his body. When she finished she proceeded to beat him with a mop handle.

Grandpa, helpless in the sheet sack, twisted and squirmed, croaking, "Now Ida Mae, don't hurt me anymore, please don't hurt me. I promise I won't do it again!"

As far as I know, Grandma never did hurt Grandpa again and they stayed married for many more years.

Bertie, 5 years old with her Grandmother and Grandfather Tracy

Bee, Bertie's mother about the time she married P.G. Anderson

Chapter Seven

Mama's brother, Dick, met P.G. Anderson when they were in Army boot camp at the start of World War II. Dick learned that P.G was from the Weed area. While looking at family snapshots together, Dick pointed to one and said, "Those're my sisters, Beatrice and Virginia."

P.G. pointed to Mama and said, "Boy, I'd like to meet that one."

Dick laughed and said, "I don't think so, she's married to a big son of a bitch and has three kids."

Later when they both spent their furlough in Weed, Dick did introduce P.G. to Mama. She was still married at the time but her marriage was falling apart and she would be divorced before she saw P.G. again.

After they divorced in 1943, we struggled to get by on the money Daddy sent and the little help Mama's family could spare.

That same year P.G. received an early medical discharge from the Army because of a broken hip that did not heal properly. His courtship of Mama began when he dropped by the house one day to ask about news of Dick. After inviting him inside Mama was apologetic, "I'd offer you a cup of coffee but I ran out a few days ago." P.G. guessed correctly that coffee was not the only thing we were short on when he saw our meager meal of biscuits and beans.

"Would you mind if I go to the store and get some coffee and a few groceries for you?" P.G. asked politely. Mama wanted to refuse the offer but concern for her hungry kids overrode her pride and she responded with a blush, "I guess that would be all right."

He went straight to Goss's store and bought a bill of groceries for us. This act of generosity and concern won over Willie, Jessie, and me instantly. It was also the beginning of a brief courtship that ended in marriage. Grandma and Grandpa Counts had not yet left the area so the day they got married P.G. and Mama took us kids to their house to stay the night. They did not have a car of their own so their friends, Rordan and Rosalie Bevels, took them to Alamogordo where a Justice of the Peace performed the ceremony. They had very little money so a honeymoon was not even a consideration.

P.G. had a great sense of humor inherited from his father, Drewy Anderson. In his younger days, Drewy "cowboyed" with Will Rogers in Oklahoma. The story goes that after Will became a well-known performer, he sent a man to Weed to persuade Drewy to join him in Hollywood. Drewy, having ridden his horse to Weed, listened to the proposal and said, "As much as I would like to see old Will, you tell him I just can't leave Delia and the kids to go on a wild-goose chase."

P.G. learned from his parents the importance of loyalty. He never looked sideways at another woman after he married Mama, and P.G. tried to provide for us. But he took no responsibility for our discipline; that was left to Mama. He made it clear that honesty was crucial to integrity, and said many times, "You are only as good as your word." He was an honest man.

P.G. was soft-hearted. Although he drank his share, he didn't turn mean, and was usually jolly. He could see humor in nearly everything and used it to his advantage. The sky was the limit when it came to making other people laugh or making them the brunt of his practical jokes. Mama would scold him for his childish behavior on our behalf, but secretly I believe she was amused by it.

When they were first married, Mama refused to drink with P.G. and she tried her best to discourage him from tipping the bottle. However, as the years wore on, and she wore down, she gradually found herself giving in. She didn't drink as much as he did mind you—but more than she should have. Her mistrust of men prompted her to stay close by his side whether it involved manual labor in a sawmill or going to the bar on Saturday night. She considered herself equal to any man and, even as she approached middle age, continued to prove it.

P.G. kept strong ties to his family who had always lived on the 360-acres homesteaded in the 1800s by his maternal grandpa Strang. The farm lay in a valley with pine and pinion trees covering the mountains that bordered the fields. The hillsides were green and after a rain, the air smelled fresh. He had no desire to leave his family or the Sacramento Mountains in spite of the hardships of trying to eke out a living in the area.

Times were hard during the war. P.G. sought whatever odd jobs he could find and that meant we were always on the move. From time to time, during the first three or four years of their marriage, between jobs, our family stayed with P.G.'s mother, Delia, on the farm. The length of our stays varied from a week to a couple of months, depending on P.G.'s jobs. While living there, P.G. took whatever odd jobs he could find and worked around the farm when he was not otherwise employed. Mama loved and respected Delia and helped her with the chores and meals. She was grateful for Delia's generosity and they never had a cross word.

The intermittent times we spent with Delia on the family farm were some of the best in our lives for in her home we were warm and had plenty to eat compared to our world of desolation, cold, and nothing to eat but beans. She would meet us at the front gate with a welcoming smile. "How are y'all doin'? Come on in and I'll fix you somethin' to eat." Those became our favorite words.

Willie, Jessie and I spent much of the time outside playing and exploring. While the boys were interested in stink bugs, spiders and other insects, I was more inclined to pick, smell, and study the shapes and colors of wildflowers. When there was a breeze, the pine trees made a comforting rustling sound that I loved to listen to as I watched the branches gently sway.

We still had no electricity or indoor plumbing and the water came from a cistern by the back porch and it took a lot of elbow grease with the hand pump to fill a bucket.

Delia cooked huge meals and made biscuits that she baked in the oven of her wood cook stove. They were delicious with her fresh churned butter. As we hungrily watched, she would make a little extra dough and brown it on top of the iron stove then she would divide the pancake among us kids for a snack before supper. It was heavenly. Although Delia was not one to show affection by hugging, touching, or using words of endearment, she demonstrated her love by providing shelter and food and these things made us love her.

She also made her own soap, which was the custom in those days, from rendered fat and lye. Each batch was cooked up outside in a huge black iron pot. To get the process going Delia would stir up the troops.

"Willie, you and Jessie carry some chunks of wood to the back yard and we'll get a good hot fire goin' under that old iron pot. And Bertie, run get me some matches to start this fire, and put that can of lye down, you'll burn yourself."

To me, Delia was the most comforting figure in the world, in her cotton print housedress, apron, her heavy flesh-colored stockings, sensible lace-up shoes and her ever present cotton bonnet. She was a symbol of stability that was otherwise often absent in our lives.

Delia could ride a horse or hitch a team as good as any man. She had this in common with Mama—both could stand their own against a man. Each day we enjoyed hearing her read the Bible. She took living by its commandments seriously. I know of only one time when she displayed anything other than patience and goodwill. That was when her beloved Tom, a yellow tabby, who spent many contented hours on a cushion beside her chair, sneaked into the chicken house and killed her freshly hatched baby chicks.

Delia's response was unexpected to say the least. She marched around the house to the front porch where old Tom lay sunning himself. My brothers and I watched speechless as she yanked him by the scruff, proceeded directly to the woodpile, and grabbed the axe. Her next action was so swift we had no time to protest—she threw the cat across a stump and chopped his head off. "You son of a bitch," she muttered, as she walked away, "You won't be killin' any more of my chickens."

I felt sad for old Tom and wished Delia had given him another chance. But our food source had to be protected. Needless to say, Delia, commanded respect from everyone who knew her. When she told us kids to jump, we sprung high as frogs.

Drewy died in 1943 of kidney disease leaving Delia a widow. Because I was the only girl, I was allowed to sleep with her at night. It was heavenly to sink into the softness of the feather mattress and inhale the aroma of line-dried sheets. I liked being covered with her artful patchwork quilts made of their many shapes and colors. I was always careful not to flop around in bed for fear she would take away permission to sleep with her.

There were many things to do on that farm, from swimming in the earthen stock tank to carving stick horses from limbs off the old apple trees. Willie and Jessie and I were always careful to carve our very own "brands." In spite of the bellyaches they caused, we would eat green apples with chips of salt from the blocks of salt meant for the livestock.

Sometimes while staying with Delia, P.G.'s brothers, Darrel and Doyle, lived there as well. Everyone had to help with the chores and the jobs included chopping wood, milking cows, gathering eggs, hoeing corn and butchering hogs. Hoeing corn was a hard, hot job and we *all* had to help so that we could can corn for the winter and roast ears in the summer. We also had to store some corn in cribs for feeding the farm animals.

One of the chores assigned to my brothers the summer of 1944, when they were seven and nine years old, was to herd the grazing milk cows from the mountainside to the barn where they would be milked before supper. One evening, after Willie and Jessie had been gone a long time gathering the cows, Darrel, said with a mischievous grin, "Wouldn't it be funny to scare those boys a little bit?"

Ghost stories, told around the fire at night instilled us kids with a healthy fear of the supernatural. With this in mind, Darrel hatched a plan that he was sure would scare the wits out of my brothers. He cut eyeholes in an old worn sheet and then snuck up the hillside to the grazing area. He found himself a hiding place behind some boulders and when my brothers and the cows came into view, Darrel rose from the rocks and began to wail and moan. Apparently he sounded more like a demented lunatic than a ghost.

Not easily frightened, Willie recognized something familiar about the raving apparition. He turned to his startled brother and grinned.

"Jess, that's just ol' Darrel under that sheet." With that, the boys began pelting the sheet-covered fiend with rocks. Jessie's deadly left-handed aim found its mark several times, and a bruised Darrel ran down the path with his hand on his head yelping, "Stop! for God's sake stop, it's me, Darrel!" He ran so fast his sheet tripped him up. When he stood and began running again, the eyeholes had shifted out of place, rendering him temporarily blind. For the rest of the way down, Darrel stumbled and rolled and fought with that sheet. Not surprisingly, Willie and Jessie made it back to the house first and they regaled Delia, P.G., Mama and me with vivid descriptions of what happened. By the time Darrel limped in, bruised and rubbing the knots on the back of his head, he was greeted with good-natured taunts. That night he made good use of Delia's homemade liniment.

#

We had a pair of stubborn mules that were the source of amusement as well as pain. Although they were Jennies, the term used for female mules, their names were Buck and Rowdy. This left us to wonder if their previous owner was blind or just resented names usually assigned to the female weaker sex.

Buck and Rowdy hauled heavy loads around the farm. One day, after the mules pulled several loads of posts to a spot where P.G. and my brothers were putting up fencing, they unhitched them and climbed up to ride Buck and Rowdy home. Taking the rutted dirt road, the easiest route, they didn't see a problem with leaving the harness chains dangling in their wake.

P.G., following closely in the old Model A, became impatient. The mules and riders needed to get a move on or get out of the way. The Model A had "occasional brakes" and no horn so he banged on the outside of the door shouting, "Hurry it up, boys, you got chores awaitin'."

The noise and hollering spooked the mules, and Rowdy, Jessie's mount, started to buck, kicking her back legs high in the air.

"Hold it, Rowdy," Jessie cried, but he was already tossed off and headed for hard ground.

"Don't run over me," Jessie screamed at P.G., knowing all too well the failure record of the Model A brakes.

Jessie grasped the dangling harness chain and hung on with all his strength. The mule sped up, dragging him along the rutted bumpy road—all the way back home.

Physically, Jessie suffered only scrapes and bruises, but his pride was more seriously damaged by the family's laughter. At times like those, Jessie missed his Daddy even more. Hollan would never have laughed at him.

Our daily lives on the farm were a constant source of entertainment and fond memories for me and my brothers. Mostly because my folks did not drink at Delia's because she did not approve of it. The birth of baby pigs and calves and the hatching of chickens were exciting but the arrival of a new horse was really special.

Darrel bought a fine looking sorrel gelding with a white blaze face and stocking legs. "Rooster" stood over 16 hands and regarded the world with unusually intelligent eyes. Although attempts had been made, he had never been broken to ride. One night at supper Darrel confidently announced, "I've decided I'm gonna start breakin' old Rooster in the morning." We all looked forward to watching Darrel's attempt to gentle this fine looking animal.

After breakfast the next morning, we could hardly wait for the big event when Darrel would climb aboard Rooster.

Pushing away from the table Darrel boasted, "The show's about to start, folks." We cleaned our plates in a hurry and dogged him to the corral, not wanting to miss even one second of the action.

A lean-to shed, used for milk cows, bordered the corral. Its roof angled low toward the back. Out front it was high enough to allow clearance for a horse and rider. Inside were four stalls, each gated and opening into the corral.

We kids and grownups climbed up on the corral fence to watch the show. First, Darrel lured Rooster with a bucket of fresh molasses grain in order to slip a rope around his neck. All the while, Darrel kept sweet-talking Rooster in soft reassuring tones.

"Easy there, boy, easy." As he crooned, he eased a saddle blanket on Rooster's back. Next, just as gently, he managed to throw on a saddle and tighten the cinch.

Rooster snorted and looked wall-eyed back over his withers at Darrel, who seemed to have lost just a little bit of his confidence. Finally, Darrel got his left foot in the stirrup. Old Rooster was whirling in a circle. Darrel swung his right leg over and took a deep seat. The show did indeed get started. Rooster lowered his head, farted and started jumping like a frog. He bucked and snorted his way around the corral until he came to an open gate leading into one of the milking stalls. With no warning, he made a sharp right turn into the stall, which was empty except for a milking stool.

"Oh, shit!" Darrel bellowed. He clung tightly to Rooster who bucked into the back of the shed. Afraid of getting thrown off, kicked, and trampled in the close quarters of the stall, Darrel hung on precariously. Every time Rooster bucked, Darrel's head and shoulders were rammed into that low hanging roof. The pounding abuse Rooster inflected continued for what seemed like an eternity. Finally he lunged through the gate and with one super-horse jump, unloaded the battered and bruised Darrel onto a large mushy cow patty.

The milking stool in the stall was left splintered and broken with legs that wobbled much like Darrel's.

In spite of his injuries Darrel vowed, "Someday I'll break that red son of a bitch." Eventually he did and rode Rooster everywhere.

One day, carrying Delia's grocery list in his pocket, Darrel rode him from the farm over to the sawmill commissary. Darrel tied Rooster to the hitching post and went inside to shop. When he ambled outside with a burlap sack of groceries, his horse was nowhere in sight.

"Damned if someone ain't stole old Rooster!"

The sawmill was located over the mountain just south of Weed. Aiming to outsmart the thief, Darrel muttered to himself, "I bet that damned horse thief is headed for Weed."

He hitched a ride in the back of a pickup and arrived at Cordelia's Bar in search of his horse and the reward of a cold beer. "I'll be damned if I wudn't right," he grumbled, as they pulled up in front of Cordelia's. There stood Rooster tied to the bar's hitching post, twitching his tail at the abundant and annoying flies.

With or without provocation, Darrel loved to fight. The theft of Rooster was certainly more than enough to provoke righteous anger in Darrel, who hopped from the bed of the pickup, took the stairs in threes, and tossed his sack of groceries on Cordelia's porch.

"You thievin' son of a bitch, what are you doin' with my horse?" he shouted, stomping toward the bar's lone customer.

Darrel's first punch hit home, but the thief stood tough and defiant.

"Well, you ain't got what it takes to get him back," he smirked. "'Sides, I just borrowed him."

The two men lunged at each other, and ended up tangled on the barroom floor. In the writhing and confusion, Darrel mistakenly grabbed his own foot, tugged off his boot—and then realized he could use it to wop the thief into submission.

Victorious, Darrel took possession of Rooster, swilled a beer, tied his sack of groceries to his saddle, and proudly rode home.

We loved living on the farm but occasionally I got bored staying at the house while Mama and Delia were busy with cooking, canning and cleaning. To get me out from under their feet Mama would insist Willie and Jessie take me with them when they went off to explore the countryside. In turn, my brothers grew weary of having me tag along, trailing them like a blood hound, and reporting back on all our activities, Willie found a solution when he noticed some prickly pear cactus growing near the edge of the cornfield.

"Hey!" he said, "there's a prickly pear! Boy, those things are good to eat."

He carefully removed a fruit and peeled and ate it, as though it were the best tasting delicacy he had ever tasted. I took the bait, and I could hardly wait to gobble one down.

"Get me one," I whined, "get me one." He carefully picked one just for me. Instead of peeling it, he plopped it into my open mouth spines and all.

"There ya go," he said pleasantly. But I was already screaming as the tiny cactus spines dug into my tongue.

With my tongue protruding, I ran crying and babbling to the house mumbling, desperately, jumping up and down, pointing to my swollen, stinging red-hot tongue.

When Mama figured out what I was trying to say, she marched me to the front porch, and with bright light and tweezers, was able to extract the spines.

After that I didn't rejoin my brothers, who were not punished. Mama figured correctly that they were fed up with my tattling tongue; and, for once, were able to silence it

"Don't get in the tank, 'cause it will muddy the waters and the cows won't drink it," Mama repeatedly warned us about Delia's earthen water tank. But the water was so tempting on hot summer days. On one such day in mid August, we were playing near the tank, busy catching horned toads. We liked to put them on their backs in our hands and rub their soft bellies. They closed their eyes and were perfectly still as though in a trance. We would then let them go and watch them scurry to freedom. By noon the temperature had become increasingly hot and we finally surrendered to the lure of the tank's cool water.

Wading around the muddy edge of the water Jessie observed how good the black mud felt as it squished between his toes. "Boy, it's fun to make tracks in this goop."

"Yeah I bet it would feel good to wade in the water a little bit too," I agreed. We discussed the matter and finally decided to take the plunge. We voted to leave our dry clothes on the bank. That way, we could put them back on after our adventure and no one would know what we'd been up to. That settled, the three of us stripped down and waded right in.

"I can teach you to float on your back," Willie promised, "just let me hold you up out of the water." I had fun up until he let go and I sank into the muddy water. After coughing and spitting out the stinky liquid, I was more than ready to go to the house.

Our plan almost worked; although our clothes didn't give us away, our red eyes, sunburns, and mud-spattered hair did. Mama lined us up along Delia's picket fence, and then she silently paced in front of us like a drill sergeant. After an eternity, she stopped. "Do you think you need a spankin' for not mindin' me?"

My brothers whimpered, "No, ma'am," eyes down on their muddy feet. I, however, hadn't really experienced much of a spanking and, feeling bad for all of us, said "Yes." The punishment must not have been too harsh because I can't remember it. But I vividly remember the dread at being found out and having to answer to Mama.

I loved helping Delia. After she put fresh warm milk into the machine that separated it from the cream, she would then churn the cream into butter in her old fashioned churn with the wooden handle that lifted the agitator up and down. When the cream turned to butter, she would scoop it into a wooden rectangular box that formed it into pound blocks. Sometimes I was allowed to do the churning.

Delia had an old washing machine powered by a gasoline motor. It sat on the back porch, along with two tubs for rinse water. I liked the smell of the soap and bluing used in the wash, and I was fascinated with the way the clothes were fed through the wringer and dropped into the tubs of rinse water. I could only watch because Mama was afraid my fingers would get caught and pull my arm into the wringer. I did get to help her hang clothes on the line to dry afterward. I would hand her items from the laundry basket and she would secure them to the line with clothespins.

Delia's cellar smelled delicious from the apples, onions, and potatoes she stored. I didn't go there often because I was afraid of the spiders that hid in the dark. But, the smokehouse's aroma of bacon or ham always made my mouth water and it wasn't as scary as the cellar.

Delia led a life devoid of frills. Her only indulgence was a flower garden by the side of the porch. It was tightly fenced to prevent her chickens from destroying it. She had to carry buckets of water but managed to grow some beautiful hollyhocks and morning glories that climbed on the old picket fence. The colors in her flowers appeared vibrant against the graying wood of her house and fence. As a result of these early visuals, hollyhocks are one of my favorite flowers.

Willie and Jessie liked to sneak into the corral and ride Delia's calves. Mama warned them many times, "Don't be ridin' those calves, you might get hurt and you'll ride the fat right off of 'em." Like all other warnings, they paid no attention. One day they came up with a new idea; one that included me. They figured if I were an accomplice, I would be less likely to tattle or maybe they just wanted to have as much fun as possible before Mama lowered the boom. Either way, I was glad to be included.

Delia had an Angora goat that ran with the milk cows. One of the cows, called Heart, had long scary horns and an equally mean disposition. She was named for the shape of the white spot on her face, certainly not for her aggressive attitude. I was terrified of Heart.

That morning the boys kept the goat in the corral when they let the cows out to pasture for the day.

"Boy," Willie said as he eyed me. "This goat has the softest hair I ever felt."

"Let me touch him," I pleaded.

The boys held onto the soft, fluffy, luxurious mohair goat. Happily stroking, I murmured, "It feels so soft."

In a persuasive tone Willie assured me, "It's even softer when you sit on it."

The gate was closed, so the goat couldn't join the cows. I felt perfectly safe in allowing the boys to set me astride the goat to feel for myself just how soft he was. However, before I could get a deep seat, Jessie, ambled over to the gate, swung it open and shouted, "Turn 'er loose!"

The goat bolted and I clung with both hands to his coat, laughing as it bounced along. Swiftly he carried me toward the open gate. The closer we got to the gate the more terrified I became for I knew that goat was headed for the cows. My fate, at the end of Heart's horns, was not looking good. My giggles turned to screams. "No, no, no," I yelled, "make him stop."

The only thing to do was to dive off the goat's back onto the soft corral ground; otherwise, I would land on the rocks in the path leading to the pasture. I dove and fell headfirst into a fresh cow patty.

My tattling tongue was in overdrive when I got to the house. "Mama," I cried, "look what they did to me," as I swiped at the green stinky mess that covered the front of me. I was no longer green with envy at my brothers' calf riding experience—just green with cow dung.

P.G. Anderson, Bertie's stepfather, shortly after marrying her mother, Bee

Chapter Eight

When I was growing up we lived in several different houses, shacks, and tents in and around Weed. In the winter of 1945 after spending several weeks at Delia's P.G. got a job at a small sawmill near the tiny village of Sacramento, about four miles from Weed. We moved into a very small "shotgun" shack that was about the size of a railcar. It must have been better constructed than some we lived in because I don't remember being as cold there. Our shack, along with the others housing sawmill workers, sat on a rocky hillside, among pine trees, with a rutted dirt road winding up the hillside from one home to another. It was very difficult for my pregnant mother to care for three children, cook on a wood stove, and keep the place clean without the convenience of running water and electricity. A lesser person would have complained but my mother never did.

The birth of my sister in that shack impacted my life and changed my place in the family forever. My reign as the only girl in a family of boys came to an end and put me second in line for my stepdad's affection. My role as spoiled little sister changed immediately to that of surrogate mother.

The day Phyllis was born would turn out to be long and painful for me as well as for Mama on her birthing bed. Early that morning, P.G. anxiously left on horseback to fetch Doc Shields, who would deliver Phyllis.

Delia had come to our house to help the Doctor deliver the baby. "You kids are going to have to stay outside and play today," Delia told us as she sat by Mama's bedside. I knew we were going to get a new baby that day. I just didn't understand the impact it would have on my own little world.

Jessie and I played peacefully for a while that morning until we became bored and started bickering. "Don't touch me anymore," he warned, picking up a discarded wine bottle from a pile of rocks. I couldn't resist the dare and poked him lightly with my finger.

He swung the bottle to warn me off—just as I bobbed forward—and the bottle smacked my nose. The pain was blinding and the sight of my own blood terrified me. "You've killed me, you've killed me," I screamed.

While I was howling, Willie knocked on the back door and asked Delia, "Can we have a wet rag for Bertie's bloody nose?"

Delia handed Willie a wet rag. "Try to get them to quiet down," she scolded, "the baby's about here."

Willie tried to console me as he cleaned my bloody face. Jessie showed no signs of remorse. "She caused it," he accused. "She wouldn't keep her hands to herself."

I was still in a foul mood when we were called inside to meet our new sister. I was further wounded when P.G., who had always showered his attention on me, proudly announced, "Come look at my new baby girl!"

Upon seeing his "new baby girl" for the first time, I scowled. "She sure is fat and bald," I pointed out. I had a beautiful curly mop of hair and hoped Phyllis's baldness would make her less loveable. That hope was dashed. My parents adored her. My jealousy grew as fast as her hair. But in a short while my unconditional love for Phyllis completely replaced that jealousy.

A few days later, Jessie stirred up a wasp's nest in an old stump. One of the enraged insects flew into his ear and stung him. I was still brooding over my bloody nose, so I couldn't feel very sorry for him.

"Mama it won't stop buzzin'," Jessie wailed, shaking his head and screaming. Mama was used to her children's disasters by now. She calmly poured mineral oil in Jessie's ear and extracted the wasp with tweezers.

A few weeks after Phyllis was born, a neighbor gave Willie a black and white spotted puppy that we became very fond of. We were playing outside when we noticed that Willie's new puppy was frothing at the mouth and staggering around wildly. We knew this was a sign of mad dog disease. Willie grabbed me by the arm and yelled at Jessie who had reached to pick the dog up. "Don't touch him, Jess. Let's get inside quick." We ran into the house, slamming the door behind us.

"I think my new puppy's gone mad, Mama. He's slobberin' and walkin' funny."

Mama looked out the window, and then she nodded. "You're right, Willie, and you know I'll have to shoot him 'cuz it's rabies."

Tears streamed down Willie's cheeks. "I know Mama," Willie whispered. "He's real sick and it has to be done."

Mama rose from her chair where she had been nursing Phyllis. She laid her on the bed. Then she turned to Willie, and hugged him to her. "I'm sorry," she said softly then went to the closet where she took out P.G.'s 30-30 rifle.

"You kids stay right here." She walked to the back door. A few minutes later we heard the gun shot.

Later that day we spent hours playing King of the Mountain on the tall sawdust pile at the sawmill. It was safe, clean, and fun to climb to the top and roll down the sides. It helped us forget for a while about our dead puppy.

Our parents worked hard; P.G. at the sawmill, and Mama cleaning, cooking and caring for us kids. They had little time or energy to play with us. For entertainment, our parents would sometimes get together with another sawmill family to play music and listen to Fern and Dessie, a singing sister duo.

"Don't those girls sound as sweet as angels," Mama would say, as she patted her foot to the beat of the music. "Yes," we would chorus, as we listened enraptured. The music provided escape from the reality of our meager life.

One time we were treated to a Christmas program at the little church in Sacramento. Oren Peck was an old bachelor who never drove a car but instead rode his horse everywhere he went. Because he was a big jolly man with a beard, he was asked to play Santa Claus following the program. At its conclusion, everyone remained seated in excited anticipation of "Santa Claus" who was to emerge from the tiny closet-sized back room.

Old Oren Peck must have been struggling with his Santa suit in the dark when he fell over some old boards and boxes of junk. The audience was startled to hear a tremendous clatter and thud as Oren hit the floor. Instead of the expected "Ho, ho, ho," what we heard was a loud, "Goddamned son of a bitch," followed by a low groan of pain.

We all sat wide-eyed unable to suppress our laughter. Some parents clamped their hands over their children's ears. Oren finally limped into the room, tears trickling down his plump cheeks. He greeted us with a weak, "Ho, ho, ho."

I'm sure many kids had their image of Santa Claus shattered or considerably altered that night. As for me, at six years old, my older brothers had already dismantled my belief in him. By mutual agreement Oren never played Santa again.

When I was seven, the job at the sawmill ended. P.G. went to work for the Calkins family who had a vegetable farm and a small sawmill. He helped them with their cabbage harvest and cut logs that he skidded off the hillside to the sawmill using a big gray work horse. We got awfully tired of eating all that cabbage P.G. brought home from the fields. It took years for us to learn to like it again.

We moved into a two-room log cabin on the Calkins property. My folks slept in the smaller room. The larger one served as the kitchen and another bedroom: where my brothers and I slept opposite the wood cook stove and table. For light, we had one coal oil lamp, which sat on the table. Willie showed us how to make "shadow animals" by holding his hands in different positions as the buttery lamp light cast shapes onto the cabin wall. A trick he learned from P.G.

It was in this snug log cabin that Mama announced, "We are going to have another baby." I was still getting used to having Phyllis around but took the news in stride.

Early on September 17, 1946, the day Reita was born, I was sent to stay with Francis Calkins, a teenager who made up a story about Reita's origin that I knew was untrue. She said with the utmost sincerity, "Bertie, your folks found a baby in a cave, brought her home and named her Reita Kay."

I liked the attention Frances paid me, and didn't want to risk alienating her by challenging her story. With wide eyes I nodded and said, "Oh, that's wonderful."

I knew that once again, Doc Shields, had helped Mama deliver to us another little sister. Although I didn't know the mechanics of making a baby, I knew they weren't found in caves.

Mama was only twenty-seven years old and had five children; the last two were born only fourteen months apart. She was worn down. Caring for her family was made even harder by our harsh living conditions and no modern conveniences such as running water and electricity.

For the first few weeks Reita cried a lot. Finally, Mama discovered there were not enough nutrients in her breast milk and Reita was crying from hunger. So she had to put Reita on a bottle. The bottles we used were not regular baby bottles. They were beer bottles with nipples stretched over the tops. We used a funnel to pour the whole cow milk into the bottles. Part of the reason we used beer bottles was that when a baby bottle became empty, Phyllis would break hers by hurling it to the floor. Because we didn't have extra money to buy bottles to keep up with the breakage, mama decided to use empty beer bottles. They were free and certainly plentiful at our house. Mama gave up on weaning Phyllis from the bottle because she was too close in age to Reita. Phyllis would sneak up to where Reita lay nursing her bottle, patting her and whispering, "kitty, kitty" then she would ease the bottle from Reita's lips and plop the bottle into her own baby mouth. Because she was only fourteen months old when Reita was born, Phyllis had little time to be the baby of the family. She didn't get the attention she needed and deserved.

"You kids take Phyllis out to play with you," Mama would instruct. "But be sure she doesn't get hurt."

Phyllis wasn't a problem for us kids. She was easily entertained. But because Mama was busy with Reita and P.G. was putting in so many hours at work, Phyllis must have felt unimportant. There was just not enough attention to go around. Phyllis seemed overly solemn. Pictures of her early in life, more often than not, depict an unsmiling child who inherited Mama's beauty and temperament.

My brothers and I spent much of our time outside, engineering in the earth bank on the hillside behind the Calkins cabin. We "drove" our homemade wooden trucks on our newly constructed "roads."

"Bertie, don't step on that road," Jessie would order, "Willie and I just made it." Not wanting to upset them, I would gingerly step over the tiny ruts.

Jessie and Willie got a pet pig from Nona Calkins in exchange for crawling into the narrow space beneath her house to drag out a wild house cat.

Jessie, who viewed most people with suspicion, later said accusingly, "The old bat just wanted to see me and Willie get bit and scratched. And she didn't want that runt pig anyway." The wild house cat battle was soon forgotten, and we all loved the little runt pig we named "Jenks."

Jenks played alongside of us, rooting the ground and grunting contentedly, as we drove our homemade trucks, and constructed shelters from tree limbs covered with pine needles. The only one who didn't like Jenks was our year-old sister, Phyllis, who toddled around on chubby little legs trying to avoid it. When she had a biscuit or other food in her hand she would hold it above her head to keep it out of our pig's reach. If she ever squatted down, however, she was fair game: Jenks would charge and root our wobbly sister over, seizing the food from her fat little fists, leaving her crying in the dirt.

We only lived in the cabin a few months when we were told we would have to move to the Snyder Sawmill where P.G. was now going to work. Tom Donaghe, a friend of our folks, came over to move our meager possessions in his old truck. Willie caught Jenks, and was about to put the squirming pig in the truck when P.G. gave us the news: "We can't take that pig with us, so Tom's gonna take him home."

We hugged Jenks goodbye, assuming that Tom understood he was a beloved pet and would keep him for us. We later learned that Tom butchered him. We cried and cried and could never stand the sight of Tom Donaghe after that; his long nose just seemed to grow longer.

P.G. went to work for the Snyder Brothers lumber mill, which was the largest industry around Weed, and we moved into yet another sawmill shack. This one had three rooms, and like the others in which we had lived had no indoor plumbing or electricity. Our water was hauled from the sawmill well in barrels and then siphoned into buckets as needed. At night, we used a kerosene lamp for light. When we woke in the mornings, we could see daylight through cracks in the siding. On very chilly winter mornings, while we were getting ready for school, snow would sometimes accumulate on the rough pine floors.

Moving from one dirty shack to another must have been difficult for Mama, but she never showed her disappointment. She just kept trying to make a home for us regardless of our dilapidated surroundings.

Just help me unpack the pots and pans," she would say, as she dug through cardboard boxes for our foodstuffs. We can't eat 'til I get a fire goin' and somethin' to cook on."

Her courage, the pungency of the wood fire, and the smell of hot biscuits and potatoes filled us with warmth and the sense that everything would turn out all right.

Just keeping us fed and our clothes washed was a full time job for Mama. She had to scrub our clothes on a rub board in a tub. She would always warn us, "You change those school clothes when you get home from school, or you won't have anything to wear tomorrow." Willie, Jessie and I rode the bus to school. No fuss was made over our grades so I don't recall if they were good or bad.

Mama was a steady image of strength, and our love for her grew as did our trust because she portrayed an image of strength. The hard life she led, coupled with her unyielding resolution, molded a woman who would not back away from any challenge. She never started trouble, but when it came her way, she faced it head on. She always said, "I'm just as mean as I have to be." And she was.

Mama detested gossips, liars, thieves, flirts and pretentious people. Murderers never made her list because she thought some people deserved to be killed—especially those who beat their own mothers or hurt little kids. She believed people should pay for their actions. She did not think the law should be involved in most situations; rather, that the individuals involved should settle their own differences. *Without* legal intervention.

She said more than once, "Only a cowardly son of a bitch has to call the law. All that does is make a lot of lawyers rich."

Mama's rules were simple. Although we heard plenty of profanity, we were not allowed to use it. We saw people drink but were not allowed to sample. Same with smoking. She would not tolerate lies, thievery, or deceit. She taught us to be proud, not arrogant, and forbid us to make fun of those less fortunate.

We were not the only ones who endured the drafty cold of the sawmill shacks on winter mornings. All the families living in company housing suffered the same fate. P.G. told the story of Lem Goforth, a fellow sawmill worker, who heated his shack with an old wood stove.

Lem came to work one frosty morning walking straddled-legged, his face filled with pain, and a blister on his bulbous nose. The blister on his nose accounted for a good part of his pain, but what caused his curious walk stayed a secret.

Uncovering the truth required masterful interrogation by P.G. "Now come on Lem," P.G. coaxed, "tell me what happened to you. Whatever it was must have been awful."

After much prodding, Lem confessed. He got up early and started a fire in the wood stove. The fire quickly burned hot, heating the surface of the stove as well as the stove pipe that vented through the roof of the shack.

Lem, in his long handle underwear, stood close to the stove, bending forward, warming his hands. He didn't know that the back flap of his underwear had come unbuttoned and was hanging down. His old hound dog, Skeeter, saw the opening as something to be investigated. When he sniffed with his cold nose, the startled Lem jerked forward. As Lem thrust out his hips, his most prized possession escaped the front of his underwear and pressed directly on the hot stove. The searing pain caused Lem to jackknife the lower half of his body away from the stove only to have his nose hit the red hot stove pipe. The result was a brand for all the world to see.

"By danged," Lem swore, "I used to like ol' Skeeter a lot 'til he poked me like that." From then on, Lem Goforth's fellow workers referred to him as Limp Goforth.

We lived so far from medical assistance, that unless our injuries were life threatening, Mama dealt with them as best she could. One day after I climbed down from the school bus, and in my hurry to get to the house, I accidentally ran into the barbed wire that was stretched between posts by the shack to serve as Mama's clothesline. Because it was a face wound, I bled profusely.

I ran crying to Mama, who was changing Reita's diaper. "Bertie, it's going to be all right," she reassured me. She soaked up the blood with a clean diaper, sterilized the wound with alcohol, and then taped it together with the hope it wouldn't scar too badly. After many years the scar finally faded.

We were generally healthy and fought colds and childhood diseases with home remedies. We shared these ailments just as we once shared our bubble gum. I remember one piece of gum that was passed around for at least two weeks before someone either swallowed or misplaced it. "You lost it, you had it last," I said to Jessie.

He shook his head adamantly. "Last time I saw it was when I stuck it in the knot hole on that pine tree by the back door."

Life in the sawmill camp was both difficult and uneventful. The work was hard and P.G. came home tired and dirty every evening and Mama was worn out from trying to keep the house clean, cook, and run after Phyllis and Reita. They chose to seek relief by having a lot of beers on the weekend. One Sunday, however, we were treated to an unusual event in the home of another sawmill worker. P.G. suggested, "Let's go over to the Henry's house to listen to that black man he smuggled out of Mexico. I hear he can't talk English but can sing it real good. Old Henry heard him in one of those bars in Juarez and brought him home to listen to."

It turned out that the man did have a wonderful voice as well as a happy smile and could indeed play the guitar and sing beautiful songs. He sang many tunes popular at the time including the famous "Mona Lisa" that we requested over and over. I never learned what happened to that man but I will never forget his singing.

Our family didn't like living in close proximity to the other sawmill families. Mama had never been one to visit with neighbors. "I have better things to do than sit around 'jacking my jaws' and listening to 'idle prattle'," she would say. For the most part she didn't enjoy the company of other women. P.G. enjoyed her company more than that of other men, and we kids enjoyed each other.

P.G. loved us and tried to not to show a preference for Phyllis and Reita although he was at odds with Jessie from time to time because Jessie had a rebellious streak. He even got into a fight with a neighbor man for threatening to whip Willie and Jessie.

Around this time, P.G. was hired to cut posts and build fencing for John and Paul Moss who owned a ranch in Perk Canyon, above the sawmill. The house they furnished us was known as the Walsom Place and was surrounded by pine covered mountains. It was fairly remote, with few neighbors, but we happily settled in. It was one of the more enjoyable times of our childhood because this was one of those times that my folks didn't drink much. Our school bus driver was a fellow student, John Dick Grissick, a senior in high school whose family lived at the end of the bus route.

While living on the Walsom Place we would occasionally hear a mountain lion squalling at night. Mama would reassure us, "There's nothing to worry about." But images of being attacked by a mountain lion still frightened us.

I liked the house on the Walsom place because I had a tiny room of my own. That summer while Jessie and I visited Daddy for a couple of weeks, and Willie stayed and helped P.G. cut posts, Mama made me a dressing stand out of wooden boxes and a stool from a wooden keg. It was a lovely surprise to come home to. Mama didn't express feelings with words so this was her way of telling me she loved me and was glad I was back home.

I loved my room except for the uncovered opening into the attic that was a black gaping hole in the ceiling. My overactive imagination kept me awake many nights when I had visions of unholy monsters hiding in the dark recesses of that attic.

One night, I could stand it no longer and crept from my bed to the boys' room and carefully shook Willie so as not to wake Jessie. I shared my fears with him when I whispered, "I think there's something in the attic above my room, I keep hearing noises."

"It's probably that packrat that left the silver spoon in the drawer the other day," he said sleepily. "You better go back to bed, 'cause if you wake Mama up she's liable to move your bed in here." I didn't want to give up my room so I went back to bed, squeezed my eyes tight, and tried to ignore my fears. I hoped it was the packrat and that he would bring us something else nice.

Mama would get up early every morning to cook breakfast and fry potatoes on a wood stove. She would then put the potatoes and biscuits into the one-pound Folgers coffee cans we used for lunch boxes. We looked forward to those times when we were lucky enough to find fresh venison instead of potatoes, in our lunch cans.

My brothers especially enjoyed living on that old place where they found many things to occupy their free time. They built a trap door in the roof of the chicken house to spy on imaginary invaders. Much to their disappointment, these assailants never materialized. They also enjoyed their fort, dragging their bedding there to sleep some of the summer nights.

Our water supply came from a natural spring that fed into a ditch. The ditch ran alongside a ravine next to the old house. It was my brother's job to locate any gopher holes along the ditch and fill them with dirt so the water wouldn't escape and run into the ravine.

One day the boys discovered what they thought were dinosaur bones protruding from the bank of the ravine. Because this twenty-foot bank was steep and difficult to climb they were forced to enlist my help.

"Now Bertie, You ain't gonna get hurt 'cause we won't turn you loose." This promise was made as they tied a rope around my waist and repelled me down the bank. "You just dig those bones out and hold on to 'em, and we'll pull you right back up." I trusted Willie completely and tried to bring back something of value but without success.

There was a wooden water trough that crossed the ravine to a ditch in front of the house. Phyllis was about two years old at the time and loved to take her clothes off and get into the ditch. One day she slipped outside, crawled into the trough and was halfway across the deep ravine when Mama discovered her. Mama was terrified that Phyllis would try to stand up in the trough and fall over the side. But she stayed calm.

She started talking softly to Phyllis. "Baby, don't stand up. Stay right there." While she distracted Phyllis, Willie crawled out to bring her to safety.

That summer P.G. brought home three orphaned baby squirrels from where he was cutting fence posts. "I think their mother was killed," he said, handing them to Willie and Jessie who put them in a pen out back. The mean little Stevens' boys were at our house the next day and let the squirrels out when Willie and Jessie weren't watching. My two brothers searched in vain for them. The next morning Willie ran into the house and breathlessly told us, "You won't believe where those squirrels are, Mama. They're in the nest with that old yellow cat and they're nursin' right along with her kittens."

The baby squirrels did fine and grew up acting a lot like cats. One of them was killed by a slamming screen door while trying to get inside the house. Another was accidentally smothered while sleeping between Willie and Jessie on their narrow bed. The last one retreated to the cellar to build a nest and was still there when we moved from the old house.

That fall, P.G. and the boys had a particularly disgusting experience. After working hard all day, they stopped by the house of J.D. Stevens and his German wife, Amanda, who was known for her dirty housekeeping. When P.G. greeted Amanda he saw that she was cutting meat from a deer hindquarter that was hanging on the back porch. He also noticed with disgust that there were maggots hatched from the blowfly on the carcass. He assumed she was cutting away the bad parts of the meat but was still queasy from the disgusting sight.

When J.D. asked them to stay for supper and have some of Amanda's stew, P.G. declined. "No, thanks, J.D., we'll just wait 'til we get home." He sent a subtle message to the boys by squinching his face when J.D wasn't looking at him. But the boys didn't get it. Jessie looked pleadingly at P.G. and said, "But we're hungry." Willie nodded in agreement and said, "Yeah, it's been a long day; can't we please eat?"

Backed into a corner, P.G. was forced to accept the invitation. "Well, I'm not very hungry," he said, "but I will have a little of that bread pudding."

He sat there feeling bad that the boys weren't aware of Amanda's unsanitary practices but believed he was relatively safe with his choice of the pudding. His illusion of being exempt from her unsavory cooking habits would soon be shattered. As he was spooning out a hunk of bread pudding, he stopped in mid-bite at the sight of a glob of hair in his pudding. He quickly stopped eating and hurried the boys into finishing their supper. "We better get on home, Bee's gonna wonder what happened to us."

On the way home, P.G. told my brothers about the meat and the pudding. They had to stop to puke along the side the road, and vowed never again to eat anything that woman cooked.

Phyllis, Bertie's sister, wading in ditch at Walsom Place

Chapter Nine

We lived from one job to the next and moved from one place to the next. There was no assurance from day to day as to how long the work would last. Living from hand to mouth did not allow us to put anything aside for a rainy day. Every day was a rainy day—with no umbrella. Any glimmer of optimism was overshadowed by the ever gathering clouds of grim reality.

P.G., who had grown up on his family's farm, was by necessity, versatile at carpentry and repairing machinery with minimal supplies and tools. Bailing wire and rusted bolts were his best friends. He never saw a nail he couldn't straighten and reuse. He could wiggle, jiggle, cobble, paste and patch hell a mile with the best of 'em. Had we lived in a more prosperous area, he would have been easily employable. But the small farms and ranches around Weed were worked by the people who owned them and were not productive enough to warrant hiring outside help.

When the job of building fence for the ranchers was over, P.G. searched in vain for another job in the area. There was no work to be had so, at the urging of his friend, Tom Donaghe, we moved to Artesia, New Mexico where P.G. worked for a man who moved houses.

P.G. was nothing if not resourceful. He bought an old faded red boxcar that had belonged to the Atchison Topeka and Santa Fe Railroad and with the help of his employer, moved it onto a lot on the outskirts of town. He then converted it into living quarters for the family with its five-foot white letters "ATSF", proudly displayed on the side. Boxcars are built for hauling heavy loads and this one was no exception; it even had hardwood floors. P.G. cut openings for windows and put up partitions to make a small bedroom for us kids. Our folks' bed was in the other room, along with a cook stove, table and chairs. Even though Mama suffered from sinus headaches at that time, she kept the small quarters neat and clean. We didn't have the money to go to a doctor so she just applied Mentholatum ointment and took aspirin.

While we were waiting to move into the boxcar, we lived in a couple of one-room cabins belonging to P.G.'s employer. The cabins each had one small window and splintery wood floors grayed by time and use. The exterior imitation brick siding had been tortured by so many windstorms that it was peeling and flaking away. It was there that P.G.'s brother, Darrel, and his drunken pal, Babe Chandler, nearly killed Jessie.

Darrel and Babe stopped by to see our folks after getting out of jail in Artesia. They had been arrested for disturbing the peace in a downtown bar with a reputation for being not all that peaceful to begin with. Both were released from jail early because they had saved the life of their half-witted friend, Fred Johnson. Apparently Fred, highly claustrophobic from being locked up, had gotten his head wedged between the cell bars in an attempted jailbreak.

Fred had a noticeably small head, an anatomical feature that helped explain his lunacy. Maybe there just wasn't room enough inside his little skull for a sufficient blob of gray matter. He was teased by the dullards he hung around with for his looks and behavior. Often he was urged to make a fool of himself for the amusement of the foolish.

The cot Fred had climbed on to reach the window slid away from the wall just as he forced his tiny head through the bars. This left him dangling, holding onto the bars for dear life, feet thrashing like a frenzied monkey. His strength was giving out and he was on the verge of suffocation, when Darrel and Babe intervened. They held on to him until the jailer could come to the rescue.

The authorities weren't concerned with Fred's potential death. They figured it was no great loss. But the fact that it could have occurred while he was in official custody was a worry. They also decided correctly that Darrel and Babe had encouraged Fred to attempt the escape, in order to break the monotony of their jail time. To protect the reputation of the department, and save the tax payers' money, the police chief made the decision to throw all three of the louts back out of jail.

On their way to Weed, they stopped by to see us, staying in the cabin where Willie and Jessie slept. They thought it would be entertaining to see an eight year old get drunk, so they let Jessie drink some of their wine. They usually drank Falstaff beer or Jim Beam whiskey but a downturn in their finances reduced them to swigging cheap wine.

Jessie had outgrown some of the medical problems caused by his premature birth, but he still tired easily and sometimes had to rest during the day. When Willie walked into the cabin that afternoon his first thought was that Jessie was taking a nap. When he took a closer look, he realized that Jessie was unconscious. His head was hanging slightly off the mattress, his face was a pasty white, and vomit had drooled out of his mouth onto the floor.

Willie ran as fast as he could to the other cabin where Mama and P.G. sat listening as Darrel and Babe recounted their last misadventure. To help discourage the two from hanging around, Mama and P.G. were not drinking with them and besides, P.G. was supposed to work that afternoon.

"Mama, come quick!" Willie yelled. "Somethin's real wrong with Jessie, he's just layin' there."

Mama ran to Jessie and scooped him up in her arms. "Get me a wash rag, Willie." And to Jessie she pleaded, "What is wrong, baby, what have you eaten?" To the others who had hurried to see what the situation was, she yelled, "Somebody get a doctor, right now!" The color had drained from her face, which was now nearly as pale as Jessie's. P.G. ran next door to his boss's house and called the doctor.

Mama continued to caress Jessie, hold him, and talk to him while we waited for the doctor to arrive. Darrel and Babe, knowing they were about to be found out, confessed that they had given Jessie some of their wine. The doctor confirmed that it was alcohol poisoning and treated Jessie.

Mama turned on Darrel and Babe with a vengeance of a scorned mama bear. "If you two sons a bitches ever give one of my kids alcohol again, I'll kill you. Get your sorry asses out of here right now!" She was shaking with rage.

"But Bee, we didn't know what would happen," Darrel blubbered. "We were just funnin' and he wanted to taste it."

"I won't tell you again. Get out!" Mama hissed.

They left. But like curs, they would return, crawling on their bellies and begging Mama's forgiveness. Mama never truly forgave them and that was not the last time she would run them off in spite of their close ties to P.G.

Jessie did not always court trouble; it seemed to come looking for him. Just a couple days after the alcohol poisoning, he accidentally killed a turkey belonging to the boss's hunchbacked daughter. Not only did the girl bear the burden of a misshapen body, her parents saddled her with the curious name "Moody," which in no way reflected her sunny disposition. Moody, in her late teens, was blessed with the face of an angel and cursed with the body of an imp. Her temperament was so sweet and her face so lovely that one tended not to notice her poor twisted body. She took care of her turkeys and chickens with loving care. Willie occasionally helped feed her birds simply because he enjoyed her company.

The day Jessie became a turkey killer he was pretending to be an Indian hunting wild game when he let himself into the turkey pen. He had no idea he would actually hit his mark when he threw a sharp pointed stick at the turkey. It was a shock when the impaled turkey wobbled instead of gobbled and a few steps later, fell over dead as a doornail. He and Willie removed the stick and tried to revive the bird but to no avail.

"Mama, Jessie killed one of Moody's turkeys," Willie cried as he ran to the door.

"He did what? Come here Jessie Lee." Mama marched the turkey slayer straight to the boss's house to apologize. Moody made no fuss over the loss of the turkey, either because she had several more turkeys or because Willie and Jessie had always been nice to her and pretended not to notice her affliction. Mama always stressed not to make fun of people with deformities.

The forgiveness in Moody's soft blue eyes evoked a level of repentance in Jessie that a spanking could never have accomplished. "I'm sorry, Moody," Jessie croaked sorrowfully. "I'll help you do chores to make up for spearin' your turkey. I'm just glad he was that ugly one with patches of feathers missin' and not your favorite."

We lived in Artesia for a short time and while we were there the whole family hired out picking cotton to supplement what little money we had. I didn't do well. I was small and the cotton sacks were bulky. Phyllis and Reita were too little to be left alone so they sat on the ends of the sacks as my parents dragged them down the rows of cotton. None of us were good pickers and had little to show for our efforts.

For P.G, the lure of living in the Sacramento Mountains was strong. Although Mama did not share his enthusiasm, we again moved back to the Weed area so that P.G. could work in Sawmill Canyon on the old Circle Cross Ranch. At one time this ranch was owned by the famous lawman, Oliver Lee.

No housing was available at the sawmill so we moved into a tent. Actually it was one of the best tents we ever lived in. It was large, with a slab wood floor and siding that made it rather snug. There was room for our beds, a table and benches, and an iron cook stove. As with every other place we lived, Mama had a way of making it feel like home. She kept the floor swept clean, the beds made, and the "kitchen" spotless. She made do with few personal belongings. Her love for P.G. must have been strong to have lived like that.

We were six, eight, and ten that summer in Sawmill Canyon when we played among the pine trees and enjoyed our chance to run free. I particularly loved the wild flowers that grew through the pine needles on the forest floor. Even at that early age I had a deep appreciation for beautiful shapes and colors. I would sometimes bring Mama colorful bouquets of wild flowers that she would place in canning jars filled with water.

One day Willie and Jessie made a shelter from pine tree limbs with needles stacked on top. Willie decided to return to our tent to chop some wood for the cook stove. But Jessie had other plans. He liked the way the shelter made him feel hidden from the world when he crawled inside and felt so comfortable. So much so in fact, that he laid back and lit a hand-rolled cigarette he had concealed in his pocket. But he accidentally dropped the match into the dry pine needles, which immediately caught fire. The only thing he had to fight the blaze with was the pants he was wearing so he used them to smother the flames. He sheepishly returned to the tent with blackened shreds for britches. Not only had he started a potentially dangerous fire, but we had so few clothes that none could be spared for firefighting purposes.

"What on earth were you doing out there?" Mama demanded.

Jessie's pale blue eyes filled with tears as he tried to avoid admitting to smoking. "I don't know, Mama, I was just playin' and looked around and there was a fire."

Mama recognized his excuse as a lie and whooped on his bottom.

We didn't get many new clothes, and never in the summer when school was out. Once when Willie referred to his shoes as alligator shoes, I was puzzled because we could barely afford plain leather, much less ones made from alligator hide. He explained that the brogans they wore were cheaply made and the soles would sometimes come loose and could not be repaired. The only way the soles could be held in place was by wrapping bailing wire around the shoes to hold the soles to the uppers. "If you don't wire 'em together, the soles flap and snap like an alligator's jaws. That's why I call 'em alligator shoes."

The sky was the limit for P.G. who loved to pull jokes on people. He especially liked to tease Willie and Jessie. He played one of his meaner jokes on them when we lived in the big tent. The two were about eight and ten years old. He set them up by saying he heard there was a terrible new disease called "red root" going around and that it only affected boys.

"The first thing you notice," he told the boys, "is a redness around your nuts. It just gets worse and worse and starts hurtin' real bad; and then the hide peels off." They listened intently, eyes wide, horrified, believing every word.

A few nights later P.G. took advantage of my brothers' deep sleep. Having borrowed Mama's rouge, he applied it quickly to those areas that would supposedly be affected. When Willie and Jessie woke up the next morning and went out to pee, they looked down in horror at their red testicles. They raced back inside the tent and in a quivering voice Willie whispered, "I think we got the red root, Mama."

"Yeah, Mama, and I'm worse off than Willie." Jessie wailed.

When P.G. turned away to hide a snicker, Mama snapped, "Damnit, won't you ever grow up! You tell these boys what you did right now!"

P.G. confessed immediately; he was well aware of the limitations of Mama's patience where his tomfoolery was concerned. The boys' embarrassment did not end when they learned a trick had been played on them because P.G. gleefully told everyone who would listen about what he had done. I didn't think it was a bit funny and felt sorry for my brothers.

P.G.'s brothers, Darrel and Doyle, and their friends, drank excessively and spent time with our family in those early years. I did not like having them around and my brothers hated their presence and the drinking even more, because they were usually the brunt of their jokes and teasing. They would sit around smoking cigarettes, drinking beer, and laughing as they recalled their drunken exploits. For the most part we kids were ignored unless they were teasing us or asking to be waited on. The teasing bordered on humiliation and my brothers suffered the brunt of it, especially Jessie, whose self-confidence was already eroded. This teasing only intensified Jessie's longing for his daddy. Willie felt sorry for Jessie but could do little to deflect the torment.

I, on the other hand was treated like a servant, "Bertie, could you bring me a cup of coffee," or "Bertie, could you run out there and bring me my smokes?" From an early age I just tried to please others in an effort to gain their approval and attention. An effort that later come back to haunt me.

Phyllis and Reita had to show off to get attention. They were encouraged to perform. "Come on now, Reita, you can dance faster than that. Phyllis, let's hear you sing again. We won't laugh this time."

I didn't realize until later that alcohol was beginning to play a large part in our lives. During the work week there was no drinking. But on weekends, out of boredom or just the need to escape a life steeped in poverty, the alcohol flowed. Whether drinking was the result of our poverty or our poverty was the result of drinking is debatable. The fact is that a lifetime affair with alcohol was being established.

We enjoyed the mountains that summer and were sorry when we had to leave because P.G. developed a kidney disease that needed immediate medical attention. This may have been brought on by the alcohol although our parents never admitted to that. His illness came on suddenly and we left in the middle of the night with all our belongings packed in the back of a large truck with sideboards. Mattresses were stacked on top of the load so that we three older kids could ride on top. We rode fairly comfortably that cold night. We were covered with all the quilts we owned and the mattresses were soft. The truck bounced along the dirt roads as we lay on our backs staring through the boughs of the pine trees at the moonlit sky. Anxious concern for our future was our comfortless companion as we traveled throughout the cold night.

Our apprehension was well founded. Life didn't get any better when we moved to Hot Springs, New Mexico. This was long before it was renamed Truth or Consequences in honor of the long-running TV game show. We moved there for P.G. to get medical help and he was also convinced the hot springs baths offered therapeutic benefits. The fact is, living in Hot Springs would prove to be one of the toughest times in our lives. We were again forced to live in a tent—a smaller one this time.

Chapter Ten

e camped on the banks of the Rio Grande River and caught fish to supplement our food supply. That fall we ate mostly potatoes and beans and finished off the home canned corn and apple butter we had brought with us. By the first of December 1946, we ran out of money to buy butter and milk for the potatoes and we relied on chili powder for flavoring. We also used it to spice up our pinto beans.

My folks did not hide their concern over money so we worried in unison with them over our future. We never complained though because we knew it would do no good. When we weren't in school Willie and Jessie spent a lot of time trying to catch fish and I just stayed around the tent trying to help Mama with my sisters. On frosty mornings the steam from the area's hot springs would rise up like fog. P.G. visited those bathhouses for medicinal reasons; the rest of us went just to bathe.

After P.G. began to feel better he looked for work but there were no jobs to be had and he could find no steady employment. He did contribute some dollars for the family by hauling scrap iron with his brother-in-law. But we were desperately short of cash, so Mama took a job at a local nightclub rolling dice in illegal gambling games. Slot machines in New Mexico had long been outlawed but the gambling spirit could not be legislated. Those folks who liked the games enjoyed the thrill of challenging the law. The dice games were held in a smoky room behind the bar. An advanced warning system allowed the patrons to exit quickly into the alley. P.G. also earned a few bucks from the bar owner for standing guard at the door to watch for the law while the dice games were in progress. Mama always hated gambling; I expect her experience in Hot Springs may have had a lot to do with that.

A month or two later, Mama bartered better living quarters for us. In exchange for cleaning house for an elderly couple named Kates, we were allowed to live in the garage behind their house.

We older kids were responsible for caring for Phyllis and Reita while Mama was at work. We fed them supper, washed them and put them to bed. Willie, as the oldest, had most of the responsibility, which he accepted without complaint. We loved and respected him so much that we rarely questioned his supervision.

The time in Hot Springs brings back embarrassing and shameful memories. Things happened then that are today still painful to recall. We didn't realize until we moved away from Weed to Hot Springs, which was much more prosperous, that compared to the way others lived, we were really very poor.

Our parents believed that being poor was never an excuse for thievery and lying, and strictly enforced this belief with severe discipline. I reminded myself of this when I was tempted to take something that wasn't mine. The only time I ignored this rule was in Hot Springs.

I was in the second grade and my school was several blocks from where we lived and in a different direction from where the boys went to school so I walked by myself. The neighborhoods where I walked were modest but I was still envious of those who lived in real houses. On my way home from school I stopped many times to peer through the window of a small one-room grocery store. This was my hungriest time of day. I could see the groceries neatly lined up on the shelves, and near the old fashioned cash register with its ornate brass metal leaves and flowers, sat the colorful boxes of candy, peanuts, and gum. Just looking made my mouth water. I finally got bold enough to step inside the store a couple days in a row—just to *look*.

A little old man, wearing gold-rimmed spectacles balanced on the end of his nose, peered across the counter and startled me by asking if I wanted anything, I flinched and ducked my head. "No, thank you, I don't have any money today," I said, then hurried out the door.

I am not sure when I decided to steal; the idea had probably been growing in the back of my mind for a few days. I had no practice at being a thief so I was unable to conceive a good plan for stealing. I just knew I wanted one of those candy bars. The third day, as I stood eyeballing the candy, a lady came into the store and said to the old man, "Would you mind getting me some of that bologna and a pound of longhorn cheese?"

"Yes, ma'am," the old man said, wiping his hands on his white butcher's apron. He adjusted his glasses, and walked behind the meat case to slice the meat and cheese. I seized my opportunity! I grabbed a Hershey bar and slipped it into my coat pocket.

My heart pounded and my face turned hot as I forced myself to walk, not run, to the door and down the street. About a block from the store I could hold back no longer and began to run as fast as I could until I felt a stitch in my side. When I stopped running and spun around, I was startled to find I was not being followed. My stomach churned. I no longer craved the candy but knew I could not take it home. I had to get rid of it. So instead of savoring tiny bites as I had dreamed, I quickly stuffed the whole thing in my mouth. I could not bear to look at the evidence of my crime.

It did not taste nearly as good as I had imagined. My stomach felt a little queasy and my feet dragged as I slowly walked the rest of the way home. That evening I watched the faces of my family as we were eating our supper of potatoes and beans. I wondered if I looked different to them now that I had become a criminal.

From that day on, every time I heard my mama say, "I despise a liar and a thief," I would cringe and say to myself, *if you only knew*. I couldn't bring myself to tell her until I was grown and we were recalling our rough time in Hot Springs. It was only then that I told her about the stolen candy bar. The sadness in her eyes spoke volumes. She responded in a quiet voice with no trace of condemnation, "I am so sorry about that."

Another really bad memory came from not having money to buy a proper gift for the school Christmas party exchange. I was so ashamed of the ten cent gift I had to offer that I could hardly face my classmates. With my dime I had few choices, finally settling on a toy made of colored wax and filled with a sweet flavored liquid. It was shaped like a tuning instrument and when it was empty you could blow into it and create whistling sounds. Of course, the recipient of my pitiful gift was clearly disappointed. This experience forever spoiled the Christmas season for me. I know that the poor do not look forward to this holiday, dreading the disappointment it brings to those who have nothing to give.

The most shameful memory occurred that same horrible Christmas. I was seven and only in the second grade but was expected to get myself ready for school. Mama worked late at the nightclub and needed all the sleep she could get so that during the day she would have enough energy to run after two toddlers and clean Mrs. Kates' house.

That day I will never forget began when I could not get my hair to look right, so I tucked it up under a scarf that I tied around my head. Later that morning the teacher, marching us around the room, chose the ones to be in the Christmas pageant.

"Bertie, pull that scarf off. You can't wear that in the play," she demanded. I stood staring in shock and dread. Then I slowly untied the scarf. My humiliation was totally complete as my tangled hair fell to my shoulders in a stringy mess. To my further shame and misery the teacher added indignantly, "That simply will not do. You can't be in the play looking like that!" I was so overwhelmed by rejection that I sobbed all the way home. I never told Mama what happened. I understood she already had enough to worry about. I did not burden my brothers with my problems either. We just tried to get by the best way we could and help Mama with our sisters.

Mama looked very tired most of the time but she was still the most beautiful woman I had ever seen.

Fortunately we were able to move from Hot Springs to Albuquerque shortly after this happened. Our move was made possible one night when Mama found a crumpled twenty-dollar bill on the floor of the nightclub. She said to P.G. as they left the club that night, "Look what I found. We can get away from this whole "shiteree" tomorrow." No twenty-dollar bill ever looked better. When she came to my classroom to take me out of school the next day I could hardly wait to leave the place where I had endured such embarrassed.

We packed up and moved to Albuquerque where we stayed with Mama's family. They lived in a small house, but there was an adobe building out back where my brothers and uncles Murrel and Bill slept. Living with my grandparents suited me fine because I enjoyed being near Grandma Counts.

Grandma was a good seamstress and did alteration work in some of the finer Albuquerque dress shops. She made badly needed clothes for my sisters and me. I was now eight years old and loved watching her sew. I tried to imitate her by cutting and stitching the scraps of material she gave me. The best part of those times was listening to the stories she told of growing up in the Oklahoma Territory. Oklahoma was not yet a state when she was born. Most everything I learned of Grandpa's family, I learned from Grandma who did not particularly care for the Counts bunch. Naturally I liked her stories about them best because they were usually scandalous and told with open disdain.

"Tell me about Grandpa's family," I begged as we sat sewing one day.

"Well, you know," Grandma said as she cocked her head to one side and snipped at the armhole of a blouse she was making, "Old Man Counts, your great grandpa, was a mean old soul, and it's no wonder he met his maker in such a terrible way." She paused for effect. "And, Doeny, your grandpa's sister, didn't amount to much either. She was redheaded, you know," Grandma said accusingly, as though that hair color was somehow a curse. Grandma never liked red hair and didn't trust people with brown eyes. Her own eyes were blue, and she never acknowledged the red highlights in her hair. I could hardly wait for the rest of the story but Grandma had me fetch a cup of fresh coffee for her first. Then after I settled down on the stool beside her she continued.

"A mulatto named Sam Bob Jenkins wanted to court Doeny who had done Lord knows what to lead him on. You know how redheaded people are," Grandma raised her brows and looked knowingly over the top of her glasses. "Of course, your great grandpa Counts wasn't gonna stand by and let a half-colored call on his daughter. He warned Sam Bob not to be comin' around Doeny or he'd kill him. Sam Bob took him at his word. Having no intention of lettin' go of Doeny, he decided to get the drop on him. He bided his time and followed the family from a picnic. As they were walkin' down the road, Sam Bob jumped from behind a bush and shot Old Man Counts in the back. Dropped him right in his tracks."

My eyes rounded out and my mouth fell open as I lusted for more information. "What happened to Sam Bob then?" I almost shouted.

"Well, he had to serve some time but they didn't hang him." She cocked her head, looked directly at me, and said in a lowered voice. "There's more to the story that nobody else knows."

"What is it, tell me," I whispered as stretched my neck and leaned toward her.

"Just between you and me," she confided, "Years later, your grandpa and his brother, Tom, went back to Missouri and killed Sam Bob Jenkins and threw him in the Missouri River."

Stunned into silence, I sat blinking. After I had time to think for a minute or two, I asked, "What happened to Doeny?"

"Well she married someone else and had a passel of redheaded kids. She turned out to be a big fat woman." Grandma added with satisfaction.

She enjoyed telling stories as much as I loved to listen to them. I believed everything she said, including the ghost stories. Grandma was very smart and had educated herself by reading everything she could get her hands on. I admired and loved her very much.

I never liked living in towns, particularly Albuquerque. I dreaded going to school because if the boys didn't walk me home, little groups of Mexicans would throw rocks at me and called me gringo. No matter how fast I ran, a few rocks hit their mark, leaving me stinging and bruised. Negotiating was never a consideration; it seemed to be the Mexican's mission in life to terrorize me. In addition to this losing battle, I hated the school. Our poverty was emphasized by a school program in which the poor kids were sometimes segregated at recess and given a piece of fruit or box of raisins. I had too much pride and was repulsed by their charity. I still dislike raisins.

My brothers and Uncle Murrel didn't get along with the Mexicans either, but because there were three of them, they were not as afraid as I was.

"Those Mexicans keep throwing rocks at us," Murrel complained one day.

"Well, if you don't take up for yourselves, they ain't gonna stop," Grandpa allowed. "Mexicans don't respect nothin' but force. They'll run you into the ground if they think you're scared of 'em." That was all the incentive the boys needed.

The next day, when my brothers and Uncle Murrel were attacked by the gang, they fought back, hitting one member with a tin can and causing his head to bleed. That evening a tall man in a rumpled suit and low-cut shoes appeared on our doorstep.

"I'm Mr. McNutts, the principal from the school and I'm here to talk to you about your boys," the man said, stretching his neck to see the accused peering at him from the safety of the kitchen. "I want you to turn them over to me so I can properly punish them."

The unfairness of the whole situation and the intrusion of an outsider rankled P.G. He glared at Mr. McNutts and cleared his throat. "If you don't get your ass back in that school yard, and do it in a hurry," he yelled, "you are going to wind up bein' just plain "Mr. Mc.""

We lived in Albuquerque for a few months in order to finish the school year. Our time there was made bearable only because Mama's family made music and we all enjoyed listening to them. Uncle Murrel was a natural musician who taught himself to play the fiddle. At twelve years old he won second place in the state fiddling competition. He played in Dick Bill's band, which was well known in the Albuquerque area. It was a wonderful treat when the whole family went to the club one night to watch Murrel perform. In addition to watching him play the fiddle, during the band's break the chubby cook with the chocolate skin, came out from the kitchen and tap danced. He was a marvelous dancer and the crowd went wild, throwing money on the dance floor when he finished.

Murrel would later play fiddle for many well known country music stars such as George Jones, Tom T. Hall, Louise Mandrel, Faren Young, Johnny Rodriquez, and Ray Price. Mama was as proud of him as if he were her own son.

Albuquerque was no place for wild kids like us who had been free to roam the countryside all our lives. P.G. had no luck finding work there, so he decided to return to the Weed area and work in a sawmill. The day after school was out for the summer we loaded our belongings on Uncle Dick's old truck. After we said our goodbye's my brothers and I settled in the back of the truck on some bedding and Uncle Dick climbed into the cab on the driver's side. P.G. and Mama sat in the cab holding Phyllis and Reita on their laps. As we pulled away, P.G. breathed a long sigh of relief, glanced back over his shoulder, and declared, "I'd rather scratch shit with the chickens than live in this place one more day."

Chapter Eleven

$\mathcal{U}$nfortunately the only available job was at a sawmill in Monument Canyon, which was so isolated there was no school bus service to Weed. So my folks made arrangements for my brothers and me to room and board with a nice widow lady, Annie Van Winkle. Annie had a passel of kids of her own and we had fun living with the family for a while. But what we really longed for was our own stability together as a family.

I was nine years old and had just entered the third grade. Jessie was eleven and in the fifth, Willie was thirteen and in the seventh. That was the year I fell and nearly broke my arm. It was a Friday night, one of those rare occasions when we were able to go skating in the school gym. We usually didn't have the money for skate rental nor transportation to get there. But this night we had both. I was skating around the floor, slowing at the corners and daring to gain speed on the straight-aways. Halfway into my tenth lap, I was startled by a skater speeding past me and fell to the hardwood floor. I landed with my left wrist turned back in a painful position. As I sat on the sidelines I cried because it hurt so bad and I could no longer skate. It so happened that Mama and P.G had come down from Monument Canyon to stay at Delia's for the weekend. Saturday morning, with my arm still throbbing, my brothers and I walked the two miles from Annie's house to Delia's. I wanted sympathy for my arm and the boys wanted to see our folks.

As we walked along I continued to complain about the pain in my arm. "I just wish Mama wasn't so far away," I said.

"Yeah, they could'a picked us up at Annie's before they went to Delia's," Jess complained. "I guess they just don't worry about us much anymore." On that day Jessie was feeling particularly unloved and I was beginning to follow suit.

"Now Jessie," Willie reasoned, "you know they have to live at the sawmill and we have to go to school."

"Well, I don't care about school anyway and I'm tired of staying with Annie, and besides, Pete's been pickin' on me." Pete was Annie's boy who was the same age as Jessie.

"Now Jess, I saw you pick back a little bit with that left hook of yours," Willie reminded him. So, on we grumbled down the dusty dirt road to Delia's.

What I remember most about that day wasn't my painful arm, but the ache I felt to see my mother and hear her comforting voice. The minute Mama met us on Delia's front porch I melted into tears and showed her my injury. "I think it's broke," I cried.

"Let me see it," she said hugging me. I immediately felt better. I burst into tears and the resentment toward my mother for not being there for me completely vanished.

Mama dressed my injury with some kind of concoction that included vinegar, and brown paper. The medicinal affect wasn't nearly as reassuring as was her love. We stayed the night at Delia's. The next day, on their way back to the sawmill camp, Mama and P.G. dropped us off at Annie's. As they drove away my brothers and I felt abandoned.

I was still nursing my sprained arm when I went to school the next day. The teacher, Mrs. Douglas, who taught first and second grades at Weed, took pity on me. Knowing we were boarding with the Van Winkle's, she asked, "Bertie, would you like to come stay with me?"

I was surprised and flattered she would take a special interest in me, and I was tired of sharing a bed with the two VanWinkle girls and thought it might be nice to stay with Mrs. Douglas for a while. "I think I would like that. If Mama says it's all right."

Mama gave her permission. Arrangements were made, and I went home with Mrs. Douglas. For the next nine months I experienced life as I had never known it.

Mr. and Mrs. Douglas lived in a beautiful mountain home. I had my own pretty bedroom with a rug. I could take baths in a real bathtub. The first thing Mrs. Douglas did was to wash all my clothes and hang them on the clothesline. I was ashamed because she thought my things might be infested with bedbugs. Although I was no stranger to shame, it felt particularly hurtful that day as the realization of my life compared to theirs was painfully apparent.

Mrs. Douglas had gray hair but her age I could not determine. It just seemed she had always been the same unchangeable age—whatever it was. Her years of teaching reflected her solemn personality; she did not often laugh. She was respected for her strict classroom discipline by generations of students. This same rigid guidance continued in her home. She was not prone to show emotion and was more concerned with teaching me how to behave properly than showing me affection.

I learned proper etiquette, both at the table and when interacting with people. The first time she formally introduced me to one of her friends I blushed and dropped my head. I paid the price for my poor manners. The minute we were alone she scolded, "Bertie, you are never to behave like that again. When you are introduced to a person, you look them in the eye, offer your hand and say you are glad to meet them." I followed her instructions from then on.

I learned to polish real hardwood floors as well as my shoes. I had other assigned chores, and was expected to do them. Mrs. Douglas believed in hard work. I had more clothes than I ever had and learned how to properly care for them. I had jeans and flannel shirts for school and two nice dresses for special occasions. I even had an extra pair of shoes. I would often open the closet door just to look and marvel at my new wardrobe. I loved to touch the dresses and try on my patent leather shoes. As I glided around the room in those shiny shoes, I imagined how good I would look when I could dress up to go to the "box supper and cake walk."

I tend to associate different taste sensations with a specific time and place. So I think of Mrs. Douglas when I eat fresh strawberries. Those berries she plucked from her garden for her homemade jam were the best ever tasted.

For the first time in my life someone actually made me do my homework. Mrs. Douglas even looked it over after I finished. My mother had neither the time nor inclination to do this. Cooking, cleaning, and caring for two toddlers with no modern conveniences drained her energy. She thought it was the teacher's job to teach and ours to learn—without her intervention.

Christmas that year with the Douglas family brought a new experience—presents.

In my family we had always celebrated with each of us getting only one or two gifts and a sack of candy and fruit.

But with the Douglas family, there were several beautifully wrapped boxes with my name on each card. In particular I remember receiving a set of play dishes, a doll, and most of all, a baton. In early fall, on a trip to Artesia, Mrs. Douglas and I watched a parade that included a high school marching band. I was dazzled by the majorettes twirling their silver batons, and tossing them up as they turned, stepping high to the sound of the band's beat. I dreamed of owning a baton of my own. I wanted to twirl around in white boots.

The only downside to that Christmas was that it was spent with Mrs. Douglas's parents and spinster sister. They all seemed ancient to me. There was also a nagging, guilty feeling that I had received so many nice things and my siblings had not.

After Christmas, when the new school term began, my third grade teacher, Miss Angel, asked each student to bring supplies for a class project. We would need a small scrap of material and a needle and thread, the raw materials to make a stuffed animal.

Such requests in the past were always a burden for Mama because we had no money to buy extra items for school. I was always creative and enjoyed art and related subjects as this was an area where I confidently excelled. Still I was reluctant to ask Mrs. Douglas for the material, needle and thread. She found out when Miss Angel asked, "Why hasn't Bertie brought the things she was supposed to for our project?"

As we were driving home from school, Mrs. Douglas scolded me for not telling her. "I didn't want to bother you," I explained.

She looked at me and sighed. "School projects are always important, don't ever forget that." She gave me a scrap of blue denim and red embroidery thread and a needle for the project. My stuffed dog was the best in the class.

Near the end of the school year my folks moved from the sawmill in Monument Canyon to the Courtney Place and Jessie and Willie joined them. This was a good thing because the boys were tired of living with the Van Winkles. Jessie, in particular, started thinking of himself as unwanted by our folks and resented by Annie's boys. Things deteriorated to the point that after one quarrel, my brothers left Annie's house and walked the long way to the sawmill camp.

At school the boys kept asking when I was coming home. One day Jessie told me, "We are really missin' you and Mama wants you to come home this weekend." During that visit Phyllis and Reita stuck to me like glue. They wanted me to curl their hair and help them dress. It didn't seem fair that I was wearing decent clothes and shoes while my siblings were dressed in worn clothes and shoes they had begun to outgrow. Mama hugged me more often than she usually did. "Bertie, we miss you and want you to be back with us where you belong," she said. She clearly felt my place was with her and my family.

"I've been missin' you too," I said. I didn't try to explain how hurt Mrs. Douglas would be because I thought she might think I was putting her ahead of the family. I also feared they all might even think I was putting myself ahead of them. I felt guilty leaving them in their poverty to go back to a more comfortable life.

That Sunday, on the way to Weed where Mrs. Douglas was waiting to take me back home with her, Mama reminded me, "Bertie, you ought to tell Mrs. Douglas pretty soon that you are ready to come home." I ducked my head. "Yeah, I know."

When we got to the Weed store, the boys jumped from the back of the old Model A and hugged and kissed me goodbye. When Reita and Phyllis realized I was going with Mrs. Douglas they began crying and grabbing for me. I kissed Mama goodbye and felt traitorous as I walked to Mrs. Douglas's blue Chevy pickup. The sound of Phyllis and Reita crying for me weighed heavily on my heart as we drove away.

I knew I was needed to help care for them and could think of little else for days. At night, just whispering their names made me cry myself to sleep. A child's strong emotions and capacity to love is amazing.

Every day on the drive home from school I would try to think of ways to tell Mrs. Douglas that I was going back home. I knew she would be deeply disappointed in me for leaving the life she had so generously given me. But after a week of torturing myself, I finally worked up the nerve to tell her.

We had been riding along in silence when Mrs. Douglas turned to me and asked, "Bertie, what's wrong? Are you not feeling well?"

"Mrs. Douglas," I blurted, eyes downcast, "I'm gonna' have to go home to take care of my sisters."

As expected, she was very upset. To this day, I have never forgotten her response. In a flat, clear voice she said, "Bertie, you don't understand it yet, but you are making the biggest mistake you will ever make."

The next week I moved back home. This made Mama ecstatic. I think she saw Mrs. Douglas as trying to steal what was rightfully hers, one of her children. She would later say she feared Mrs. Douglas might try to force her to give me up.

The family was very excited when I returned. Willie and Jessie wanted to know everything about my life with the Douglas family. I entertained them with all the stories I could think of, especially those involving Mr. Douglas who was a wonderful man with a good sense of humor. At first my brothers were a tiny bit envious of my experience. They might have been resentful, too. They accused me of being "uppity" when I tried to show everyone proper manners.

"Sit down here," I urged. "I'll show you how to act at the table, but first you have to wash your hands."

"I'm not gonna wash my hands if I'm just gonna play like I'm eatin'," Jess said.

"OK, then, just sit down!"

I took a knife, spoon, and fork from the can in the middle of the table, and a plate from the cabinet and made a place setting. I ignored the fact that we didn't have enough utensils to properly set the table for everyone.

"You must put your napkin in your lap before you start passing the food," I said, pulling my back very straight. There may have been a tad of Mrs. Douglas in my voice. "And you should pass each bowl of food to the right after takin' some for yourself."

"It's not gonna work," Jess said, interrupting my instructions. "In the first place, we don't have any napkins, and in the second place passin' stuff that way would take too long."

"It will not take too long! That's the way you're supposed to eat, and you're supposed to ask if you may be excused before leaving the table."

"Excused for what? I ain't done nothin' wrong yet," Jess retorted.

"Jess, shut up and listen," Willie said, shaking his head. She's trying to tell us somethin' for our own good."

Phyllis and Reita had joined the learning circle although they were too little to remember anything I told them. Eager to participate, Phyllis asked, "What am I 'posed to do?"

Reita, just tall enough to peek over the edge of the table said nothing. But her blue eyes took everything in. Mama, who was at work that day, was unaware of my lesson, but I'm sure she would have approved. Any improvement in her brood would be welcomed as long as it was not motivated with criticism and ridicule.

I continued to offer advice but knew the race was lost when at supper that evening an argument erupted over who would get the last biscuit. I did notice a few feeble attempts at good manners by the group as time went on. My siblings got over their envy and teasing but I never stopped trying to make things better in the family because I had learned there was a better way to live.

I brought the toys I had received for Christmas home with me but I did not play with them. I knew better. My sisters were too young to understand how to be careful with my things and I was afraid they would break my dishes and tear up my doll. When I complained, Mama said, "They're just little girls and if they see you playing with your things and cry for them you will have to let them play too."

So I carefully hid my doll and dish set, along with a large stick of peppermint candy, in the attic above my bed. The other kids had a stick of candy too, but they quickly ate theirs. I saved mine to eat one piece at a time.

During the day, while Mama and P.G. were at work, Phyllis and Reita, now four and three, usually tagged after me. They must have seen me hide my treasures in the attic. Somehow they managed to climb up on my bed, where they engineered a stack of boxes into a stairway. Balanced precariously, Phyllis then hoisted Reita up onto the rafters. Reita soon uncovered my stash. She then passed my treasures down to Phyllis. They broke my dishes and left my doll out in the rain. They also ate my candy.

I was very angry when I saw what they had done and even angrier that Mama didn't see fit to punish them. Mama reminded me that they were much younger than me. My brothers said I shouldn't have been hording my candy in the first place.

"We were tired of hearing you gnawing on your candy at night," Jessie said. "Yeah," Willie agreed, "All that smacking kept us awake."

In spite of all this, I never once regretted coming back home to my family.

Phyllis was four and Reita three and both were nearly inseparable. It was my job to watch them. One afternoon, not long after the destruction of my dishes, toys and candy, they decided to make mud pies, a favorite past time.

They were out behind the house, ankle-deep in mud, "baking" pies and smearing their little bodies with mud "frosting."

Reita wound up with a good amount in her hair. Phyllis decided the best way to deal with her sister's dried mud was to make it disappear. She found a pair of scissors and reassured Reita, "I'll fix it, Weita, I'll make it all gone." She cut Reita's hair in chunks down to the scalp.

Our teasing caused Reita to be aware and self conscious of her thin straggly hair. We had no idea the cause of it was probably due to poor nutrition. I once pointed to the shadow it made sticking in every direction. "Look, Reita," I said, my voice taunting. "Your head looks like a porcupine."

Reita turned, saw her odd prickly shadow and she began to cry. Her tears made me ashamed, and I never teased her about her hair again.

On occasion Phyllis helped Reita with her hair problem by hanging Mama's cotton panties on her head to simulate hair; unfortunately, the panties weren't always fresh from the drawer. Mama didn't mind as long as they were entertaining themselves.

When I rejoined the family, I had to get used to the increased responsibility that was heaped upon me. Mama felt an obligation to help P.G. earn money to support us even when it required her to take jobs usually reserved for men. Our parents hired on at a little sawmill that was about three miles from the house, so during the work day, my brothers and I were expected to watch after Phyllis and Reita.

Mama did the cooking when she was at home, but when she was at the sawmill I was expected to get supper started. Because of our poverty we had few ingredients to work with, and Mama was forced to serve her family basic fare. She never had the chance to experiment with new and varied dishes. As a result, cooking was not something Mama learned to enjoy. Rather, it was undertaken for the sole purpose of filling the stomachs of five kids and two adults. Exciting our appetites was not a consideration, and I cannot recall any of our hungry pack being picky or fussy about food. We understood there were no options and—table manners be damned—eagerly consumed whatever was placed in front of us. I cannot remember actually going hungry although we rarely experienced much variety in our meals.

Our diets consisted primarily of pinto beans, although, on occasion, we were lucky enough to have lima beans or black-eyed peas for variety. Another main staple was potatoes—usually fried; sometimes with onions added. Some years Mama canned corn, tomatoes, apples and jellies. The fruit and jellies never lasted more than one season. In the interest of time and ease, Mama rarely made yeast bread but rather baked quicker and easier biscuits or corn bread.

We couldn't afford beef except for an occasional bit of hamburger. We raised some pigs but our primary meat supply was venison, mostly from deer killed out of season. Some people ate poached eggs; we ate poached venison and were damned glad to have it.

Sometimes we were lucky enough to buy whole milk from people who owned cows. Otherwise we made do with canned milk diluted with water. Our potatoes, beans and onions were kept in burlap sacks in the corner of the kitchen.

Added to the difficulty of cooking with so little for so many, the old house where we lived had no electricity, running water, or fuel other than wood. Because we had no refrigerator, perishable items were kept in a window cooler that sat outside the kitchen window. It was a large box with a metal bottom that held a couple gallons of cool water. During the day, we placed dampened burlap sacks over the cooling box so that any breeze could penetrate the wet sacks and cool the contents. The box opened into the kitchen; when we wanted to take out milk or meat, we simply pushed aside the small curtain or screen that served as a door.

The kitchen had a cabinet for dishes and a small counter for preparing food. There was an equally small wash stand, a pan for washing and a communal towel that hung from a nail. We shared a dipper to scoop drinking water from a bucket. We sat on benches and stools around an oblong wooden table. Our eating utensils were stored in a can, set in the center of the table, alongside salt and pepper shakers. At meal times, each family member chose his or her preferred utensil. My brothers and I usually picked knives and forks while Phyllis and Reita were allowed only spoons. My previous lectures on table manners did nothing to alter this procedure.

I cooked on a wood stove with help from my brothers who chopped the wood and started the fire in the firebox. Maintaining an even temperature in a woodstove was difficult at best, it required turning the damper, and letting the fire burn down, or adding wood for more heat. To keep the food from burning, we moved the cooking pots around on top of the stove. It was a full time job, demanding the sleight of hand of a shell game con artist. Keeping a close eye on the oven's food was a must because there was no temperature control.

Our potable water was hauled in barrels with bungs for siphoning from the sawmill well. Open-topped barrels were placed strategically under the eaves of the house to catch rainwater runoff from the roof. This water was used for washing dishes and bathing.

Kitchen scene just before Jessie set curtains on fire at Courtney Place

At the sawmill Mama worked long hours alongside P.G., and I felt sorry for my beautiful mother. I was more than willing to help the family. The boys cut the wood, carried the water, and generally helped watch after our little sisters. I feed them leftovers for lunch and got supper started before Mama and P.G., exhausted and dirty, came dragging home from the mill.

One perfectly beautiful summer day, I was watching my little sisters while they played with stray kittens and baby chicks. We did not have many toys but the animals made fine substitutes for dolls and teddy bears—they were soft and cute, made noise and could run. Mama did not like cats and would not allow them in our house. They had to stay outside and tolerated only if they were good mousers. So my little sisters could only play with them inside the house when Mama was away at work.

We had a few baby pigs. But because of the mean disposition of the old sow, we seldom laid hands on her offspring. If we wanted to, someone had to distract her with a bucket of slop while Willie or Jessie, the fastest, and most surefooted, scrambled into the pigpen and grabbed a squealing little pig. No matter how you tried, though, the pink little devils squealed nonstop and the old sow became, more and more aggressive. The risk of life and limb for a squealing, wiggling mass of muscle and fat just wasn't worth it unless there were visiting kids to impress.

One summer day my brothers decided to go rabbit hunting. Before they left, Willie carried in a bucket of water, then asked Jessie to bring in a couple of baby chicks and a kitten for Phyllis and Reita to play with. Jessie quickly responded as he was always anxious to go hunting.

At lunch time I buttered some cold biscuits and put a dab of syrup on them. Then after dampening a wash rag, I turned to the girls. "Let's wash your face and hands before you eat."

Reita held up one of the chicks. "Here, Bertie, wash his face too." She laughed while I pretended to do just that and I lifted her up on the bench to eat lunch.

"My baby wants some milk, too," Phyllis said pointing to her kitten. I poured a little milk into a saucer and the kitten hungrily lapped it up. Phyllis giggled and munched on her biscuit.

The day continued peacefully including the girls' afternoon nap.

I was not a very good cook and had to start supper early. At nine years old, I was unable to shape biscuits, so I made what we called "bachelor bread." It was made from biscuit ingredients but with a thinner consistency and poured into a greased pan. When it was done we sliced it into squares. I peeled the potatoes as carefully as I could, keeping in mind that I mustn't waste any. The boys were back from their excursion on the hillside, and Willie had loaded the firebox of the stove with kindling. Once the fire was blazing, he added larger chunks of wood. He tended the flame, working the damper until it was enough for a cook fire.

"Okay, Bertie," he said, wiping sweat off his face. "I'm goin' back out to feed the sow and chop some more wood."

I mixed the bachelor bread, poured the dough into a greased bread pan and put it in the oven. I then placed a skillet on the stove with bacon fat. When it was good and hot I poured in the potatoes, now sliced and rinsed. They popped and sizzled as I stood by with my spatula. I added water to the pot of beans left over from the night before, stirred them and set them to warm on the stove behind the skillet of potatoes.

While I tended supper, Phyllis and Reita entertained themselves with their chicks and kittens. Jessie, the troublemaker, was standing at the open window. He had his back to me and something about his posture made me suspicious. I tried to get a closer look, but when I moved, he moved too, until his head grazed the flimsy curtain at the window. He was cupping something protectively in his hands. As he glanced over his shoulder, his pale blue eyes darted slyly. That's when I saw the hand-rolled cigarette dangling foolishly from his lips, and the burning match in his hand.

The curtain, lifted by the breeze, billowed softly and just that quick caught fire from Jessie's match. Flames quickly shot up the wall. They singed Jessie's white hair and eyebrows, and he began to slap his head screaming, "Oh, my God, I'm on fire!"

When Jessie realized the curtain was burning, not his own skin, he lunged into action, grabbing the straw broom and beating the flames. But the fire had spread to the wallpaper. At this point, the door opened and Willie came in the kitchen carrying an armload of wood. When he saw Jessie and the blazing curtains, his eyes went wide. He dropped the wood and it scattered across the kitchen floor.

"Bertie," he yelled, "get the girls out of here!"

While I pushed Reita and Phyllis toward the other room, Willie grabbed the bucket of drinking water and tossed it on the flames.

We were very lucky because the bucket was almost full. Willie and Jessie then managed to put the fire out. They tore down what remained of the curtains. I huddled in the other room with Phyllis, who was holding a kitten tightly to her bare little chest, and Reita who was clutching a half-smothered chick in her dirty little hands.

Once we realized we were all unharmed, we remembered that Mama and P.G. would be home any minute. We tried frantically to clean up the mess. I grabbed the broom and swept the dirty water and scorched pieces of curtain out the back door. Willie barked out orders, "Put those chicks in the hen house, Jess, and Phyllis, you better put that kitten back outside."

Phyllis, still frightened, tossed her kitten over the porch rail. "Out you bits," she shouted, mimicking what she thought Mama had said when she tossed the old mother cat out the night before.

In the chaos of the fire and attempted cover-up, I burned the potatoes and bread and scorched the pot of beans I was warming for supper. Any hope Jessie had of getting away with smoking his homemade stogie went up in flames along with the curtain. His deed was evidenced by the scorched wall, bare window, and stench of smoke hanging heavily in the air and there was also his singed hair and eyebrows screaming for justice.

Mama grabbed Jessie who yelped and howled as she whopped his backside for sneaking around smoking and setting the house on fire.

Poor little Phyllis, anxious to help in the cover-up, didn't notice that her kitten had landed in the half-filled rain barrel. When its lifeless body was later discovered in the barrel, she was inconsolable. Mama scooped the kitten from the barrel and drained the water out. As it soaked into the dry dirt by the porch she sighed, "That is sure a waste of good rainwater."

I went to bed that night thankful that no one had been hurt, and that several lessons had been learned. Among those lessons were, of course: don't smoke next to flimsy curtains blowing in the breeze, and watch where you throw your cat."

We were still living on the Courtney's Place when P.G. and Mama quit the sawmill and began working for Cordelia Lewis, who owned the bar in Weed. She hired them to build a laundry. The downside to their working for Cordelia was that when they collected their pay at the end of the week, they were inclined to stay at the bar and drink. The hours of waiting for them to come home were excruciating.

One Saturday, P.G.'s brother Darrel, dropped by our house to visit. My sisters and I had waited eagerly all morning for our folks to come home so we could all be together. When Darrel showed up, they still had not come with their pay.

Darrel seemed irritated at our being left alone again. "Bertie, get Phyllis and Reita ready and I'll take you all to Weed." Darrel, like the rest of P.G's family, was fond of me and I was grateful to him for singling me out because

I was feeling neglected and unappreciated. I did the best I could to make us presentable. I put Phyllis's hair in pigtails and used plenty of bobby pins to secure the front of her hair in pin curls. Reita's hair was too short for styling. I dressed them in the only clothes that were clean—jeans for Phyllis and a dress for Reita. Although Phyllis didn't have a blouse, I was proud of the fact that both girls wore shoes.

Darrel loaded us in his pickup and drove to Weed. Somebody at Cordelia's bar took a snapshot of us as we sat on the steps in front of a storage building next door. Years later, when Mama sent me the snapshot, the words she wrote deeply saddened me. "Bertie, here is that picture you asked for. You can keep it. I don't need to look at it anymore. I have all the bad memories from that time that I can stand."

Chapter Twelve

Cordelia hired Mama to run the newly constructed laundry and she hired P.G. to build a house on one of several properties she owned around Weed. In exchange for P.G.s work on this and other jobs, Cordelia allowed us to move into the house.

Our new home bordered the local cemetery, the inspiration of seemingly infinite ghost stories. My brothers delighted in terrifying me, and they warned me about wandering outside at night near the resting place of so many dead people. They never mentioned any one particular ghost but intimated there were many and not all were friendly.

The house was a great improvement over our previous living quarters, although the drywall in the bedrooms was never finished while we lived there. It lacked indoor plumbing but it did have electricity, linoleum floors, and more room than we had ever had. Not long after we moved in, we bought a couch, chair, and an end table—the first living room furniture we ever owned. We were very proud of it.

In the past, our living rooms always served a dual purpose as a bedroom with a bed in one corner and a few straight-backed chairs around a wood stove. This house by the graveyard was much better. Some memories of our life in this house are not pleasant but mostly I am reminded of the better times we had there.

People around Weed grew up knowing just about everybody. Because there was little to entertain us, we were forced to create our own amusement. Fortunately, the area was home to a number of talented self-taught musicians. Listening to them play was great fun, but dancing was even better.

We had what we called "home dances." One family or another would clear out their living room furniture, except for chairs around the wall, and roll up the rug, if they were fortunate enough to have one, so that people would have room to dance. Everyone danced, including the kids. I don't remember exactly when I learned to dance; it just seems that I always knew how. It was a natural thing to join the grownups and dance until we were exhausted. We looked forward to a break around midnight when cake and coffee would be served. Those gatherings were carefree and joyous.

We used to laugh at the way Mable Burgess danced around the floor. Mable was a well-endowed woman whose enthusiasm for dancing infused every inch of her generous body. As she fast-stepped and circled around the floor she would flop her arms to the beat of the music. In fact she looked very much like an old hen flapping and stretching her wings.

Although she never knocked out a partner with her vigorous arm pumping, she came close. Not because she had a mean hook, but because she didn't like wearing deodorant. The resulting puffs of sweaty odor sidelined more than one hearty male dancer.

As the evenings wore on, some of the adults drifted out to their cars to sneak sips from the liquor bottles they had brought with them. I'm not sure what all the secrecy was about because it was perfectly obvious by their dance style (or lack of it) who had indulged. Sometimes Mable's partners appeared to have imbibed more than the others, possibly in an effort to deaden their senses.

From these home dances I learned how much fun dancing can be.

One of my classmates from Texas, Doris Phelps, whose father worked at the sawmill, had taken tap lessons before moving to Weed. I was fascinated by her dancing and told Mama, "I know I can learn to dance like Doris. All I need is some tap shoes."

"Bertie, we can hardly afford school shoes," she responded, "much less dance shoes."

"Well, I have that old pair of sandals, Mama, all you need to do is nail some taps on 'em."

I don't know where Mama got the taps, but she did, and after she nailed them on my shoes I asked Doris to teach me some basic tap dance steps. Every day at school recess she patiently taught me to tap dance. We only had a rocky hillside where our house sat, so I would walk over to the school yard with its cement sidewalks and endlessly practice. I tapped along the walks, around the cistern, up and down the steps, and back again; over and over. In addition to what Doris showed me, I tried from memory to imitate some of the steps I'd seen the cook in Albuquerque perform. At home, I liked to dance to the rhythm of "Chattanooga Shoe Shine Boy". When I tapped to the scratchy record on our wind-up record player, the wooden floor vibrated causing the needle to skip. This meant I was out of step much of the time—but that did not stop me. My determination was unwavering.

When I finally learned to tap dance well enough to keep up with Doris, we performed in a school program. Both of us wore skirts made of white and red crepe paper. Doris was the star because she was the better dancer, but boy, I was proud to be in those hillbilly follies. The joy I felt made me understand why that colored cook, I had watched so long ago, seemed so happy while he danced. I felt if I worked hard enough I could do anything.

Mama worked very hard all her life, and running the laundry for Cordelia was no exception. She helped people operate the old wringer-type machines, and she also took in washing and ironing for the more affluent customers. She was always tired when she came home. One morning, in a hurry to get to work, Mama accidently let a red-hot skillet slip from the stove. Bacon grease scalded her foot. That was one of the few times she ever saw a doctor. P.G. drove her to Alamogordo for emergency treatment. She came back home and tended to the burn herself. I remember her grimacing in pain, tears running down her face, each time she changed the bandages. Mama had to use crutches for several weeks but still managed to run the laundry because we needed the money. It's little wonder that she and P.G. sought refuge at Cordelia's bar on many a Saturday night.

Mama used printed flour sack material to make dresses for Phyllis and Reita on a treadle sewing machine. She salvaged enough of the same print to sew for my two sisters because they were small and didn't require much yardage. She sometimes also ordered material out of the Montgomery Ward catalog.

She was excellent at upholstering. Unfortunately she used these same techniques when sewing dresses for me. They felt comfortable only if I kept my arms at my side and didn't move my shoulders—much like a mannequin. This encouraged me to learn to sew my own clothes at a very early age.

I learned to sew on Mama's treadle Singer sewing machine when I was eleven. The first outfits I made were Halloween costumes. I cut up old curtains and sewed them for my sisters and me. That Halloween the whole family went to a home dance, dressed up and wearing masks. Willie and Murrel helped make the music that night and we had a terrific time.

One of the greatest gifts in life is the unselfish love of a good dog. We had some fine dogs in our lives and loved them all. But none was so cherished as our wonderful dog, Sarge. We found him wandering along the highway between Hope and Artesia. Jessie, who loved dogs better than he like most people, spotted him first. "Look at that dog runnin' out here in the middle of nowhere," he yelled. P.G. stepped on the brakes and backed up for a closer look. The minute the pickup came to a stop, Jessie jumped out and started calling to the dog, "Come here, boy, come here." With his tail between his legs Sarge cautiously approached Jessie. He looked hungry and when he bowed his head, Jessie reached out and stroked him. Sarge received the caress gratefully and showed his appreciation with a wag of his tail. "Could we please take him with us so he won't starve," Jess pleaded. We sensed there was something special about this wandering canine, and with my folks' approval, Jessie loaded him in the back of the pickup.

The pads on his feet were bloody from running in the rocky desert and he thirstily lapped the water we poured from our canvas water bag into an empty coffee can. Our new dog was grateful but not greedy for the scraps of biscuits we shared with him. We guessed that Sarge had been an Army guard dog because of the tattooed numbers in his ear. During World War II there was a military installation not too far from Roswell, New Mexico, which was rumored to have been a German prisoner camp where guard dogs were used.

Sarge was a beautiful mixed breed with brindle colored curly hair, a white collar and markings similar to those of a collie. He was smart and loved the family, especially Jessie. He and Jessie were inseparable and spent many hours playing and roaming the hillsides.

We had an old 1934 Model A pickup that looked like it had been attacked by a mad butcher wielding a giant ax. The top of the cab had been hacked off after it was damaged in a wreck. Only the windshield had survived. For a very long time the Model A was our only means of transportation. The ease of getting in and out of this rattle trap was its best feature. If you couldn't get the door open, all you had to do was step on the running board and hop over the door into the front seat or, for us kids, into the back.

Beloved dog, Sarge, waiting for ride in 1934 pickup

One day Mama was driving this eyesore from Weed over the hill to the sawmill to haul some slabs of waste lumber to burn in our wood stoves. Jessie sat in the passenger seat fiddling with the pair of leather gloves he would use to load the firewood. Sarge stood behind the seat in the back of the Model A looking straight ahead. They were rounding a curve on the rough gravel road when the steering mechanism broke. Mama lost control and started veering off the road. "Hold on Jessie," she shouted, as the Model A lurched off the road and into a ditch where it came to a sudden stop astride a large stump.

Jessie hit the dashboard with a thump. Poor old Sarge took the worst beating of all. He had been standing astride a large chain saw in the back of the pickup. As he stiffened and squatted to keep his balance, he slid down the length of the saw raking his private parts on the teeth of the saw. With a terrified yelp, Sarge leaped from the pickup and hit the road racing for home. He slowed only once casting an accusing glance back at the Model A.

Sarge's experience in the first wreck didn't lessen his desire to ride in the old Model A. Anticipating another ride, he waited patiently in the back while the Model A was jacked up on blocks and Willie, who was fourteen at the time, made repairs.

The day the repairs were complete, Sarge danced in a circle in the back of the pickup, wagging his tail furiously, grinning and eyes gleaming with excitement. Willie jumped in. "O.K., Sarge, let's take her for a spin." Sarge, who had been ready for days, assumed his passenger position standing in the back with his head up over the back seat looking straight ahead through the dirt-streaked windshield.

In his haste to drive the pickup, Willie didn't notice that the brake fluid had leaked out. The pickup started gaining speed as it rolled down the hill. To his horror Willie realized he had no brakes. He looked over his shoulder at Sarge whose expression had turned from happy to terrified in a split second. As the old Model A bounced across the cattle guard at the bottom of the hill, running at full speed and gaining momentum he was forced to make a radical decision. To stop the runaway bucket of bolts, he steered it into an old cottonwood tree that stood beside the school principal's house.

The impact was worse than the other wreck and poor old Sarge was flipped over the back of the seat where he landed on the floorboard with his feet sticking straight in the air. He had the wind knocked out of him. Finally coming to his senses, he shook his head vigorously and frantically jumped from his death trap. Whining and yelping he staggered back up the hill to the house and safety under the back door steps. Sarge's love of riding was over. He never went near a vehicle again.

My talent for drawing was obvious at an early age. In the first grade I remember creating drawings for the other kids to color. My favorite time in school was when we colored handout sheets or in workbooks. I never asked for art materials at home. I used the backs of used envelopes or scraps of paper to draw on. I felt lucky just to be fed and clothed. Art material would have been luxury we could not afford.

The first real encouragement toward becoming an artist came when I was in the fifth grade and did a pastel painting at school. It was the first time I had ever used pastels and I became more and more excited as my painting of a Western landscape with a horse and rider began to look better with each stroke. I couldn't believe I was creating such a nice scene. I walked around the room comparing my painting to others. My heart beat faster as I realized it was the best but I was careful not to say so. Our teacher, Mrs. Reams, entered the class's artwork in the Alamogordo fair and my painting won a blue ribbon. I was bursting with pride when she handed me that ribbon, for it validated what I already knew—I was good at art. Knowing this allowed me to hope for something better in my life, something to look forward to. Having been ashamed of so many things in my life, I craved admiration and approval. Art seemed to be my best chance at achieving this.

I loved school art projects and I was very competitive. Maybe too much so. In the beginning I annoyed the other students. One day I carved an elephant from a bar of Ivory soap. It turned out to be the best carving in the class and I didn't hesitate to loudly and proudly show it around to everyone. When I came in from recess, my elephant lay, broken in half, on my desk. After that I ratcheted down my pride and tried to be more modest and less vocal about my artistic abilities.

Willie's eighth grade teacher, Mr. Angel, hired him to chop wood. On Saturdays, Willie would walk from Weed to Sacramento, chop wood all day, and then walk back to Weed. Mr. Angel was impressed with his hard work and saw a lot of potential in him.

One Saturday as they sat having lunch, Mr. Angel talked to Willie about going back to Oklahoma with his family and going to school there. Willie waited a few days before mentioning this conversation to Mama.

"Mama, Mr. Angel wants me to go back to Oklahoma next year 'cause he thinks I'm really smart," Willie said in a hopeful voice. "He says he'll help me and I can get better schoolin' there."

Mama shook her head, but didn't look surprised. "No Willie, that's just too far away." She did not consider that she was preventing Willie from having the chance to make his life better. She would not hear of Willie's leaving and although he was terribly disappointed, he never mentioned it again. Just like me, Willie felt it was his duty to help his younger siblings. But after that Willie seemed to lose interest in school.

Most of the time we stayed at home by ourselves but sometimes we were allowed to go with our folks to Cordelia's bar. The building that housed the bar had a tiny area on one end that served as a grocery store. In the middle section was the old bar with its brass railing, spittoons and benches along the wall. The room at the far end was a dancehall that had a nickelodeon in one corner and benches around the walls on which to sit. Cordelia's living quarters were in the back of the building.

When there were dances on Saturday nights we went with our folks and danced to the nickelodeon if there weren't any fiddle and guitar players around. Phyllis and Reita danced together from the time they were little and were both good at it. If they got sleepy they would either curl up on the benches or climb into the old Model A pickup.

We saw a few bar fights—usually involving just a couple of people because there weren't many extra folks around to fight. There was no shortage of fighters, however, when the sawmill was operating at its peak. The Texans brought in by the mill management were considered outsiders by the locals who viewed them as high-handed offensive braggarts. The ongoing exchanges of curses, lies and ominous threats between the two factions finally erupted into an explosive free for all one Saturday night.

On that night, Cordelia had hired Orval and Bessie Long to run the place. There were a lot of patrons in the bar, and several dancers in the dance hall. A few folks stood out on the porch, which had a wrap around railing to keep the drunks from falling off and rolling down the rocky hill. The porch stood about eight feet off the ground with wide steps leading from the rocky hillside to the building.

Earlier in the day, Mama and P.G. decided to go to the dance and told us kids we could go too. Besides us, the bar patrons that night included a tall blond man named Jessie James and his sassy redheaded wife. James was standing at the bar rail drinking beer and bragging about Texas and Texans, when he antagonized Mama, with the intention of causing a fight between her and his wife. "You better watch out," he goaded, "my little redhead just might mop up the floor with you." Predictably, Mama rose to the challenge. "I don't think so," she said, just as the bantam rooster redhead strutted up to her. She never had a chance. Because Mama always believed the first lick would win the fight. The redhead's butt quickly and decisively met the floor with a thud and Mama jumping astride her, started beating and pummeling her. Seeing his wife on the losing end, James roared over and kicked Mama in the side.

Willie and Murrel, about fifteen at the time, were watching the fight from a bench along the opposite wall. When he saw Jessie James kick Mama, Willie jumped in to intervene.

"Hey, that's my Mama you just kicked," he shouted as he drew back his fist. Willie wasn't quick enough for the experienced brawler who hit him, sending him flying backward across the room. His butt hit the floor before his boot heels did. Murrel, who had jumped off the bench to help Willie, ran into the same fist.

By this time the redhead had surrendered, Mama got to her feet, her eyes darting around the room, "Who was the cowardly son of a bitch who kicked me?"

"That man, Mama," Willie pointed from where he lay on the floor.

With that, Mama decked James with an uppercut. She always wore a large ring and it served a dual purpose that night. Not only was it a good looking piece of jewelry, it took a strip of hide off Jessie James' nose. P.G., having missed the ruckus thus far due to a much needed visit to the outside privy to relieve himself of the beers he had consumed, came rushing through the door just in time to see Mama's fist make contact with Jessie's nose..

At some point during all the chaos, Bessie Long who was helping her husband tend bar, came around from behind the bar and attempted to break things up. She slugged P.G., who had joined in and was fighting Jessie James. After her fist made a connection with P.G.'s jaw she panicked and tried to jump back over behind the bar again causing her dress to fly up over her head. P.G. made a grab for her but succeeded only in tearing the back out of her underpants. This enraged, Orval who in turn, grabbed a gun from behind the bar. As he came around the bar, Babe Chandler tripped him and the gun flew out of his hand. Willie grabbed the gun as it slid across the floor, scooped it up and ran out the front door. Carrying the gun, Willie ran across the porch, down the steps and around the building, hoping to keep anyone from getting seriously hurt with the weapon.

While Darrel was putting the finishing touches on his Texan, out of the corner of his eye, he saw Willie running around to the back of the building with the gun in his hand. He didn't realize Willie was just getting the gun away so nobody would get hurt. He took off down the steps and around the building in hot pursuit of Willie. Darrel tackled Willie and took the gun away from him, and then he hid it himself.

The fight started in the bar and had spread onto the porch and dance hall where other locals were slugging it out with their own Texan opponents. Allen VanWinkle, a very tall slow-talking fellow, and his stocky wife, Wilma, had been shuffling around the dance floor to music from the jukebox. Wilma was a mellow old gal and strong as an ox. Right in the middle of "Love Sick Blues" Allen paired off with his own Texan. The Texan's wife jumped on Allen's back and started hitting him over the head with both fists screaming, "You big bastard, you're hurtin' my man." Allen calmly looked back over his shoulder at his red-faced assailant and said in his slow drawl, "Wilma, get this thing off my back." Allen threw the Texan against the wall and proceeded to wallop him so hard that his leather jacket split right down the back. Simultaneously, old Wilma lifted the screeching woman off Allen's back and offered some good advice, "Now honey, you better behave, or I'll give you some of what your husband's gettin'."

I was standing out on the porch, looking at all the things going on around me when a beer bottle whizzed by my head. I took cover behind an old trash barrel on the far end of the porch. From there I saw Darrel, who loved to brawl, smile as he hit his Texan in the mouth. The Texan staggered backward into the porch railing and with a second blow to the chin, the fellow flipped backward over the railing, falling onto the rocks eight feet below.

My brother Jessie wasn't so lucky either; scared, he ran around behind the building and in the dark tripped and fell into a big hole that was being dug for a septic system. Willie heard his cry for help. He lay down on his belly at the lip of the hole and with an outstretched arm was able to pull him out.

For weeks we laughed, rehashed, and relished every aspect of that fracas.

All confrontations at Cordelia's were not so funny or frivolous. One time a fight almost turned into murder and our family was involved. The terrifying event happened on a school night. We older kids were to take care of our little sisters while our folks went to Cordelia's to have a beer. After putting Phyllis and Reita to bed, we went to bed and were sleeping soundly. Around midnight we were awakened by a lot of noise and the excited voices of Mama and P.G.

When we ran into the living room, the first thing we saw was blood dripping from a cut that ran across P.G.'s face. He was white from shock. Mama had him lie on the couch trying to stop the blood when Phyllis and Reita came in. At the sight of their daddy's face, they started crying. Reita screamed, "Who hurt my daddy, who hurt my daddy!" Phyllis ran over and tried to take the wash cloth out of Mama's hands. "Daddy, Daddy," she cried. "Somebody hurt Daddy!"

Being abruptly awakened at night was nothing new to us. A few weeks before, we were roused by a gunshot blast. P.G., a little bit too tipsy, was showing off and accidentally shot a hole through the roof. He claimed he was aiming at the overhead light.

The situation this night was much more serious, however, because there was so much blood.

My folks always believed that the worst thing to happen was to get involved with the law. They had never heard the old saying, "He that goes to the law holds a wolf by the ears." Theirs was a conclusion based on their experience that no good outcome can be expected when the law gets involved. This fear prompted Mama to worry aloud, "How long do you think it will take for the law to get here?"

"Probably not long," P.G. said.

While they sat waiting for the law to come, which in this case was Lawrence Barrett who was deputized to handle area disputes, they told us what had happened.

They had been drinking beer in Cordelia's bar when Clem Slugs, a sawmill camp reprobate, brought Pearly Jackson, a black man, to the bar to buy some whiskey. Segregation was very much in effect at that time and black people weren't allowed to drink in the bar although they could buy liquor to go. Clem Slugs was widely known as a troublemaker, and true to his mongrel ways, stole P.G.'s coat as he exited the bar.

P.G. followed him outside and confronted him with the theft of the coat. This led to a fistfight and P.G. knocked him to the ground. Clem then tried to lie his way out of the altercation by accusing Pearly of the theft.

"He took it. That nigger took your coat."

When Pearly Jackson heard the false accusation, he must have feared for his own safety. With a knife in his hand he came from behind P.G., reached around and sliced him across the face. P.G. jumped up, terrified he would be killed. As he whirled around he grabbed his pocketknife and slashed

Pearly who clutched his stomach and bent forward just in time to keep his insides from falling out. His legs gave way and he collapsed to the ground. Clem quickly loaded Pearly into his Jeep and drove him to the hospital in Alamogordo. Why Pearly cut P.G. is still not clear, as it's hard to believe he had any allegiance to Clem other than he had given him a ride.

As expected, Deputy Lawrence came knocking at the door. "I'm sorry, P.G.," he said, "but I've got to take you to jail in Alamogordo 'til we see if that colored man lives."

We waited fearfully for the next three days. Fortunately, Pearly Jackson lived, got well, and there were no charges brought against P.G.

Reflecting the times and attitudes toward blacks back in 1950 the judge told P.G. when he released him, "We should hang you for NOT killing him."

P.G. was greatly relieved that he had not killed Pearly even if it was in self-defense. A month later P.G. ran into him over at the sawmill. Pearly apologized for cutting him in the first place and they shook hands with no hard feelings. Then later, when Pearly was burned to death in his sawmill shack, P.G. was afraid he would be accused of setting the blaze. P.G. breathed another long sigh of relief, when the fire was ruled an accident.

These violent incidents conditioned us to become anxious and worried when our folks drank. From time to time their drunken discussions would turn into a heated argument. We never knew when it would happen. We witnessed them become physical on occasion and Mama was not necessarily on the receiving end, as she had a mean right hook.

Fortunately there are a lot of positive memories to counter the bad ones during this time in our lives. With not much in the way of entertainment in Weed, we learned early in our lives to entertain ourselves. The boys built a house in a pine tree on the side of the rocky mountain near our house, and we regularly used it as a hang out. Willie and Jessie also engineered a makeshift tram by climbing to the top of a sturdy pine and fastening the end of an old cable to its trunk. Then they unrolled the cable down the hill to a second pine tree where they again secured the cable to the top of the tree trunk. Finally, with the help of our mules, Buck and Rowdy, they pulled the cable fairly taut. With the tram now in place, Willie and Jessie would climb the uphill tree and hang a horseshoe over the cable. Holding onto that horseshoe with both hands, they would swing off the limb, and go flying hell bent for leather down the cable to the downhill tree. Because the cable had enough slack so that it dipped in the middle, the boys lost momentum toward the end of the ride, allowing them to stop without crashing. They would then grab onto a limb, scamper down the tree, and run back up the hill for their next daredevil ride.

I watched with envy as they whizzed past me, shouting and laughing all the way down. "I want to ride too," I whined.

"O.K., maybe we can fix something up for you to ride in since you ain't strong enough to hold onto the horseshoe," Willie said.

My ever obliging brothers found an old metal ring that had once held together the slats of a wooden barrel. They put the ring over the cable and fastened the ends together to form a circular seat where I could sit for the ride down the cable.

I was delighted to take my turn and eagerly climbed the tree, got into the ring and took my first look down at the rocky hillside. Then I suddenly realized how far off the ground I was and how rough the landing would be if I fell. My knees went rubbery, my arms started shaking, and I changed my mind about going for a ride.

Jessie and Willie, who had invested a lot of time and manpower into designing my circular seat, were determined to see their experiment succeed. "Let me down! I don't want to go now," I screamed. Too late. They ripped my fingers from the pine branch and shoved me down the cable.

Completely terrified, fearing if I weren't killed outright I would probably be paralyzed or brain-dead, I was on my way down for my first and last tram ride. Everything happened in such a fast blur, that I forgot what Willie and Jessie had told me about stopping: "Whatever you do, Bertie, stick your feet out in front of you, before you get to that downhill tree!"

I slammed into the tree with my knees and forehead. In my mind, I saw myself falling ten feet to the rocks below. My fingers were welded to that ring in a death grip. It took both brothers to pry me loose; they guided me, bruised, bloodied, and badly shaken to the ground. If their goal was to get rid of me, they certainly succeeded.

That spring my fiddle-playing Uncle Murrel came to stay with us for a few months. He was mature for fifteen and a bad influence on my brothers. One night when they came home early from a school function, as Mama had told them to, I overheard the three of them making an inordinate amount of noise—dropping their shoes on the floor and bouncing on the bed. Although it was freezing outside, they raised the bedroom window for "fresh air."

I was suspicious of these unusual theatrics and pressed my ear to the wall so I could listen intently. What were they up to?

Finally, I overheard Murrel's hushed voice, "I'm out, hand me my shoes." Within seconds, all three of them escaped through that window and were running down the hillside scattering rocks in their wake.

"Mama," I yelled at the top of my voice, "the boys are sneakin' out!"

She already knew. Before they had a chance to cross the cattle guard at the bottom of the hill, Mama swung the front door open wide and hollered, "Get your asses back here and into bed."

They crept back up the hill, sheepish, with heads down. I felt smug and righteous at helping to foil their getaway. They must have heard me yelling to Mama, because for weeks to come, they sought revenge. They taunted me and even bent my baton.

Although I never asked anyone to spend the night with me I was delighted when Wanda Gurley, a friend whom I admired, asked me to spend the night at her house. Her dad, Denver Gurley, was the most handsome man I had ever seen, except for my own daddy, and her mother, Odessa, was the sweetest lady one could ever meet.

The night I stayed with her, Denver drove home after tipping a few too many at Cordelia's bar. Upon stepping from his truck, he noticed Odessa's hens were roosting in the pine trees instead of in the chicken house. The sight of them perched on the pine tree branches at the back of the house must have enraged him, because he grabbed his pistol from under the seat and with a drunk, loud whoop and a holler, began target practice.

"I'll teach you chickens to roost in the hen house," he yelled. "I'll shoot your damned tail feathers off."

When his rampage was over and the feathers settled, five of Odessa's chickens lay dead on the ground. Poor Odessa, already tired from waiting up for Denver spent the rest of the night picking feathers from the murdered chickens. It is the only time I can ever remember having fresh fried chicken for breakfast. My friend Wanda seemed to take it all in stride, but Sherril, her brother was embarrassed. I had a terrible crush on Sherril and his discomfort only made me like him more. Unfortunately my love for Sherril went unrequited. My attempts to gain his attention were exercises in futility. I blamed this on shyness, considered it a challenge, and continued my campaign to make him like me, to no avail.

Occasionally the whole family treated themselves to a rodeo and picnic. This was the case one Fourth of July when we drove the Model A pickup twenty-one miles to Cloudcroft to attend the rodeo and a barn dance.

Cloudcroft was, and still is, a beautiful mountain village surrounded by tall pine trees. We enjoyed a delicious picnic that day, and then P.G. backed the Model A up to the fence that enclosed the rodeo arena. We had our own private "box seats," and after a full afternoon, we giddily arrived at the barn dance where we all danced 'til midnight. There were grown folks and little kids kicking up their heels. Just as we were about to leave, a fight broke out in front of the old barn, but for once, our bunch wasn't involved.

The grownups started home with us kids huddled under our picnic quilts in the back of the pickup. The moonlight was exceptionally bright that night, which was a good thing because the old Model A lights didn't work. To help guide our way, Mama and Mable Burgess took turns holding a big flashlight on the road in front of the vehicle. There was no traffic on the bumpy gravel road and we made it home safely. It was a good day indeed.

There is generally less chance for getting into trouble in a small village. However, this did not affect Jessie's odds for doing so. In their quest for mischief, he and his best friend, Pete VanWinkle, once stole a couple of Cordelia's chickens. They were caught red-handed roasting the chickens over a campfire. The smoke from the fire gave their location away. As punishment, and to teach them a lesson, Cordelia made them dig a water line ditch in the hard rocky hillside behind the bar.

Later when discussing the theft of the two chickens, Jessie corrected me. "No, there were twelve chickens."

"I thought there were only two," I countered.

"Well, later we went back and killed ten more 'cause we thought she worked us too hard for the first two." Whether that was true or not, I don't know. Jessie was good at spinning tales or perhaps he didn't want to admit that Cordelia got the best of him.

Jessie longed for his daddy and because of his low self-esteem and feelings of being unloved, his emptiness was replaced with rebellion. Jessie enjoyed fighting and watching fights the way some folks enjoy sporting events. There was a time or two that he manipulated Willie and me to fight others. That was, until we figured out he just wanted to watch us fight. He once asked Willie why he didn't like to fight and Willie told him, "Jess, I don't have many friends and I don't want to get rid of the ones I do have."

One such time was when he goaded me to fight Sue Goss. Her older sister, Pansy, intervened and told Jessie to stop making trouble. Jessie then went home and told Mama that Pansy had jumped him. That led to Mama having words with Pansy a few days later. Because Jessie liked to fight and got into mischief he had some sworn enemies in Weed. One was Daisy Weems, who was the aunt of Sue and Pansy Goss. Daisy owned the boarding house directly across from the grocery store. She was a large bosomed woman with a bottom to match, and knew all the gossip in Weed and generously shared it with anyone who would listen. Her saving grace was that she lovingly cared for her orphaned grandchildren. Daisy was the first to know when someone misbehaved, and, in her on-going feud with Jessie, often reported his misdeeds to Mama. This put her at the top of his list of mortal enemies.

One of Jessie's grievances toward Daisy involved our jackasses, Buck and Rowdy. He was riding Buck and leading Rowdy to water one day in front of Daisy's boarding house. She saw him coming, opened her gate and ran her Jersey milk cow out in front of them. The bell on the leather strap around the cow's neck clanged loudly. Buck spooked at the sight of the teat-swinging, bell-ringing yellow cow and tossed Jessie in the gravel road, skinning his hands and knees. Jessie, who knew Daisy had deliberately ambushed him, vowed revenge.

He bided his time and a few days later he caught a glimpse of Daisy's colorful print dress as she disappeared into her outhouse. He gathered a little pile of rocks and waited. As she opened the door to exit he started throwing his stash of rocks. She quickly stepped back inside slamming the door after her. His famous left arm did the trick and she was trapped inside the outhouse for more than thirty minutes. Daisy really had something delicious to report to Mama then. But Mama never put much stock in what Daisy said and this time was no exception, so Jessie caught a break and didn't get punished.

Occasionally, my brothers and I went to the Baptist church. We especially liked to visit when the black folks from the sawmill came to sing. They had beautiful voices singing with pure uninhibited enthusiasm whereas the regular members of the church sang the same songs over and over, almost by rote. Mama read the Bible regularly but she did not attend church. And it seemed the only time P.G. got religion was when he was drinking and became especially repentant. It made me mad to see him emotional, sometimes crying, praying and singing hymns when he was drunk. I took church going very seriously and felt he was irreverent. Later, I would come to believe that each of us should communicate with God in our own way.

At the time I did not understand my mother's negative attitude toward church people. She did not discourage us from going to services, but neither did she encourage it. Her attitude did not keep Willie, Jessie and me from occasionally going to the Baptist Church, which was just across the draw and could be seen from our house. The depth of her loathing for the law and hypocrites was evidenced once when Mrs. Booker, a member of the Baptist church, falsely accused Willie of stealing a rifle from her house. She compounded her mistake by calling the sheriff to come and arrest Willie.

Mama was embarrassed that the neighbors saw the sheriff's car at our house. When she found out that Mrs. Booker's own son had stolen the gun Mama became enraged. She had no respect for Mrs. Booker in the first place, especially after learning that she had attempted to adopt out her crippled son before moving to Weed from California. Mama viewed giving away ones child comparable to the actions of a cur dog. Mama thought Mrs. Booker was the perfect example of a hypocrite, and she confronted her on the church steps as she came out the door with a Bible tucked firmly under her arm.

"Don't you ever call the law on one of my family again, you phony hypocrite. Before you start blamin' my boy for somethin' you better look closer at your own, at least the ones you ain't got rid of yet. I hope you told your fellow church goers here that you lied about my boy and that your own is a thief." With that she turned and marched down the steps ignoring the shocked expressions of the congregation.

Our parents continued to rely on us more as we showed increased responsibility in taking care of our younger sisters. As I grew older, I helped clean the house as best I could, feeling that if I could just keep things in order at home, our lives would follow suit. It never worked.

One Saturday I spent the whole day mopping and cleaning while Mama and P.G. worked for Cordelia; Mama at the laundry and P.G. building fence. After work they stopped to have a beer. To my dismay, P.G.'s brothers and a friend came home with them at closing time and by noon the next day the house was in shambles. I looked at the spills, empty bottles, and overflowing ashtrays and went to my room where I sat down with my head in my hands and sobbed. I don't believe anyone had even noticed the clean house. But I still continued to try to "fix" things.

I was so focused on feeling sorry for myself that I did not realize the effect my parent's and relative's behavior had on my brothers and sisters. Willie and Jessie would sometimes go to Annie VanWinkle's to stay with her boys, Jake and Pete, when P.G.'s brothers and their friends, showed up at our house. Although this was embarrassing for them, Annie understood our situation. My brothers resented having to give up their beds to drunks who made rude remarks, and never cleaned up after themselves. I had no place to go to escape the situation and besides I felt I needed to be there for my sisters. Phyllis and Reita were always competing for our parent's attention so I became a stabilizing force for them. They regarded me more as a mother than a sister. In turn, Jessie and I felt the same comfort from Willie's unwavering care.

The responsibility we showed in taking care of Phyllis and Reita, as well as ourselves, made our parents rely on us even more. One winter, just before Christmas, Darrel and his wife Opal, talked P.G. and Mama into going to Juarez, Mexico with them. They were gone for several days. In their absence, P.G's mother, Delia, found out we had been left alone, and furious, she sent a friend to bring us to her house. When my folks returned she lit into them about neglecting us. That was the only time I ever heard open criticism of their behavior.

In Juarez, they had obviously blown most of their money. The only gifts they brought back were a pair of mittens for me, a basketball and gloves for the boys, and for Reita and Phyllis, two rubber dolls – black ones, because the stores were all sold out of white ones. They also brought my sisters and me some felt jackets decorated with Mexican designs. This was not one of their finest hours.

I doubt that our parents understood the extent of the anguish and despair their drinking caused us through the years. We did very few things as a family and weekends were usually spent with my folks, and sometimes their friends, drinking. Instead of spending money on something the family could enjoy, they spent what little they had on drinking. When we were younger we had spent many hours sitting in the car outside of bars waiting for them. We kept each other company, ate junk food, drank sodas, and sometimes wrapped ourselves in coats and napped. The need to use the restroom was an excuse to go inside and ask them if they were about ready to go home. The answer was usually, "Yeah, in a little bit. Go back out. We'll be there in a while." The times we didn't go with them we spent the hours at home lonely and anxious for their return. Inviting friends to our house was out of the question because we were ashamed of their excessive drinking and we never knew what mood our parents would come home in.

One of the less boring times we spent waiting for our folks was when I was about eleven, Phyllis five, and Reita four. We went to Ruidosa to watch Murrel play fiddle in a band at a nightclub. We arrived early in the day and spent the better part of it at a small bar on the outskirts of town. In searching for the restroom, we discovered an empty dance hall in back of the bar, and with permission from the bartender, we wore ourselves out playing and dancing to the music of the jukebox.

We became very creative dancers. Phyllis and Reita danced together, whirling and twirling and I danced by myself, two-stepping and waltzing with an invisible partner. We would run and slide across the floor giggling and singing to the music on the jukebox until Reita fell and skinned her knee, which I cleaned with bathroom tap water, and then applied a glob of wet toilet paper. Phyllis tore her dress when she stepped on the hem while doing a summersault, so we went to Mama and got safety pins from her purse to make temporary repairs. Periodically we went into the bar to get sodas, peanuts and Fritos. Naturally the junk food and carbonated drinks didn't mix well with flips and jostling; Reita barely made it into the bathroom to upchuck. With Reita out of commission we went to the car and fell asleep in the back seat and waited for our folks.

When it neared the time to go watch sixteen-year-old Murrel play in the band we went to the house where he was staying with the other band members. There we cleaned up a bit before going to the nightclub. We sat at the table near the bandstand and all loved the music. This treat made up for having to wait the long hours in the car.

Later that summer Grandpa and Grandma Counts came to live with us and that suited us just fine because we loved them very much. We had moved out of the house by the cemetery and into another old house while P.G. and Grandpa Counts built a small house of our own. It had no indoor plumbing or running water so we still had to haul our water and chop wood, but it was ours and we were proud of it. P.G. planned to wire it for electricity later. As it turned out we would not live in the house very long before our final move from Weed; but not before P.G. and Willie got into a serious confrontation.

Willie was fifteen, going on sixteen. He had worked hard all his life and developed into a sturdy teenager, growing increasingly tired of our parents drinking that caused so much of our suffering. One day he could stand it no longer.

It was on a Saturday afternoon. The family was sitting in the living room, except for Grandpa, who was in bed with an asthma attack. P.G., who had downed several beers, was a little high. Instead of breaking up a spat between Phyllis and Reita, he encouraged them to fight it out.

Their spat had turned into a struggle and the little girls were in a bear hug rolling around on the floor with dirty faces streaked with tears, snot and red splotches. They were tired and ready to quit when P.G. intervened.

"You two started a fight, now you can just go 'til you finish it."

"I'm tired," Reita cried, "I want to stop."

"Me too," Phyllis whimpered.

"No," P.G. said, "You ain't finished yet."

Willie stood up, an angry grimace on his face, and said, "P.G., that's not right to encourage those little girls to fight like that."

P.G. was surprised and took immediate offense that one of us kids would call him down. "Listen here, Willie, they're my kids and I'll do what I want. If you don't like it, I'll just whip your ass."

"I don't think so," Willie said as he stood face to face with P.G.

About that time Mama stepped between them and said, "Nobody's gonna whip anyone today. And Willie's right about the girls."

Phyllis and Reita had stopped wrestling and were watching their daddy and Willie with frightened eyes.

Willie stormed outside and Mama followed. It wasn't long after that that Willie went to work on the Jernagen's ranch and later moved to Artesia.

The sawmills closed down and there was once again no work for P.G.. When my parents announced we were going to move to Artesia, Jessie and I refused to go with them. I was eleven, going on twelve and Jessie was nearly fourteen. Jessie said, "You go on to Artesia and just leave me and Bertie here. We can take care of ourselves. Besides we have old Sarge here with us."

Mama argued for a while but finally relented. "O.K., you can get groceries on the bill down at Goss's and we'll be back in two or three weeks to see how you're getting along. There's plenty of wood in the woodpile. You'll just have to keep some chopped and be careful not to use too much water from the barrels cause you'll have to wait for us to get back to haul some more."

With just Jessie, me and Sarge, it was lonesome after they left. One night as Jessie and I sat playing cards by the light of a coal oil lamp, we heard a knock on the door. It startled us and Jessie checked to see that his 22 Rifle was in the corner before answering the door. It turned out to be Mama's brother, Uncle Bill who was one of our favorite relatives. He was a cowboy and boot maker who, as a conscientious objector, had spent time in an Arizona prison rather than go into the Army. It was in prison where he learned to make boots. Since his release, Uncle Bill had been working at the Jernagen Ranch, the same ranch on where Willie worked. We loved to hear him play the guitar and sing and were so excited to have company we could hardly stand it.

"Please stay all night," I begged. "We ain't had no company since everybody moved to Artesia."

"Yeah, and we ain't seen you in a long time," Jessie added.

"I'd like to stay, but I've got to get those windmill parts back to the ranch," Uncle Bill said. "Those old cows are gonna get mighty thirsty if that windmill don't get fixed." I believe he came by just to check on us since it was not out of his way to stop by.

With that, he hugged us goodbye at the door and disappeared into the dark. We were so disappointed we threw our cards down, blew out the coal oil lamp, and went to bed.

We chopped wood, used water from the barrels sparingly, cooked, and attended school every day. When my folks returned in three weeks to see how we were doing, I was so lonesome and tired of doing all the cooking that I was ready to give in and move to Artesia with them. Jessie, however, was not yet ready, and figured he and old Sarge would go it alone. Jessie stayed in Weed another month until our beloved, Sarge, was poisoned by a vengeful neighbor who didn't like Jessie because Jessie had argued with him over Jessie shooting his 22 rifle too close to his house. Jessie was completely devastated. "I guess I might as well go with you," he said with tears in his eyes, "there's nothin' left for me here now that Sarge is gone." We mourned the loss of Sarge for many years.

After the sawmills closed and there was no other work available it was obvious we would never be able to move back to Weed. On a cold day in December, P.G. and Mama made a trip from Artesia to burn the house down for the insurance money.

Weed was such a small town that their presence would not go unnoticed, so when they arrived in Weed in the afternoon they went to the house, which was relatively empty except for some old metal bedsteads and springs, an iron stove, cupboards, tables, chairs, benches and cardboard boxes full of junk. They started a roaring fire in the stove so the smoke would let folks know that they were there to check on the house. After hanging around an hour or so they went by Cordellia's bar and had a few beers. When they left P.G. told Cordelia, "I guess we'll go down and stay at Mama's and get an early start back to Artesia in the morning."

They did go to Delia's but in the middle of the night P.G. got into his black '46 Ford and took the back way toward Weed. About a mile from the village he pulled over, killed the motor, and walked to the house. It was a full moon so he didn't stumble or attract attention when he crept up the rocky hillside to the house. Inside the house he put more wood in the stove, knocked the stove pipe loose from the wall, and laid pieces of wood close to the stove. He splashed a little kerosene around and walked to the back door. Just before he exited he tossed a match into the kerosene-soaked kindling near the stove, stepped out, and shut the door behind him.

He headed down the hill toward his old Ford the same way came but with much greater speed. Unfortunately, when he looked back over his shoulder to judge the progress of the fire flickering through the kitchen window of the house, he stumbled over a dead branch under a tree and went sprawling down the rocky hillside where he came to rest on his back. This knocked the breath out of him, swelled his left eye shut, and peeled back the skin on his knees and hands from the rocks and sticks when he hit the ground. As soon as he could get his breath he lifted himself from the ground and continued his moonlight dash to the car. Mama was relieved when he got back to Delia's. She took one look at his wounds and said with a mix of sarcasm and humor, "Damn it, P.G. I thought you were goin' to burn a house down, not get into a barroom brawl."

Arson was never suspected. Everyone assumed that the wood stove had malfunctioned and burned the house down.

Chapter Thirteen

Artesia sits smack in the middle of a desert. Land not under cultivation from artesian wells—some of it prairie, most of it scrub, mesquite and cactus—is constantly at the mercy of wind and blowing sand. The wretched landscape deepened my sadness at having to leave the mountains which were home. Artesia also marks the town in my memory where our family began to break apart in a way it never had before.

Mama and P.G. rented a little rundown café on the outskirts of town on the Roswell Highway. The two of them and, for a while Grandma, shared the cooking and waiting on occasional customers who stopped in. The property included a very old motel with eight small rooms identified by faded numbers on the doors. The motel's mustard colored stucco was cracked and chipped and the wood that framed the windows and doors had not seen a paintbrush in years. Each room was furnished with a bed and dresser, sink and commode; common showers were housed in a separate building. Water stains decorated the ceiling and years of grunge soiled the walls. We moved shotgun-style into the motel rooms: Mama and P.G. in one, Willie and Jessie in the next, and Phyllis, Reita, and me sharing the third. My grandparents along with Uncle Murrel, who was sixteen, had rented a small house in town.

Moving to Artesia did not change our poverty much. Although we didn't go hungry, we barely had money for necessities much less entertainment. Jessie and I scoured the roadside and trash cans for discarded pop bottles, which we could redeem for pennies. When we had enough, we paid the fifteen cents for us and our sisters to attend the Saturday matinee at the movie theater. We would sit for hours staring up at the big screen, dreaming of lives filled with excitement and glamour. The musicals were my favorite, and my best fantasy was to be up there with the movie stars dancing in their beautiful costumes.

During those years, new clothes qualified as luxury items. My sisters and I wore secondhand dresses and shoes. Mama got some of them from a woman who ran a Laundromat and sold used clothes. One chilly day, when I could find no socks to wear to school, I borrowed a pair of P.G.'s, tucking them under at the toe, because they were much too long for my feet.

On that day Edna Pennington, a perfect little girl with bright blue eyes, asked me accusingly, "Are those man socks?" My face grew hot with shame. I ducked my head and quickly walked away, avoiding her for the rest of the day.

A couple of weeks later I was again humiliated when another classmate recognized my outfit. "Hey, you're wearing my old dress," she said, her voice blaring loud as a bullhorn.

That kind of social rejection made Jessie and me long even more to be back in the mountains. We were still grieving over the loss of our dog, Sarge. Our attempts to console each other often ended in tears. Jessie would brush them from his pale blue eyes as he remembered the things he and Sarge used to do. I would become weepy at the sight of his tears, joining him in his sorrow.

My little sisters didn't escape social rejection and persecution either.

We lived on the wrong side of the tracks. The school where Phyllis was enrolled consisted of drab ugly army barracks for classrooms. She didn't like going to classes because she was afraid of the little gang of Mexican kids who called her "gringo" and threw rocks at her after school. One day while trying to outrun the flying stones, she caught up to a couple of black girls her age who were also targets of the little mob. The girls brandished a piece of cardboard to shield their heads from the rock barrage.

"Come get behind our cardboard," one of them shouted. She had tiny pigtails tied with pink bows all over her head and it turned out her name was Jenny.

Phyllis scared and crying, ducked gratefully behind the shelter of the cardboard. "I don't know why those kids want to hurt me," she cried.

"It's cause you ain't a Mexican," explained the other little girl, whom Phyllis would later learn was named Ruby.

"We'll walk you home if you'd like," Jenny said. They did and Phyllis was grateful for the new friendship.

When she got home mama asked, "Why were you walking with those little colored girls?"

"Because they had cardboard," Phyllis explained, "and they said they would be my friend and promised to walk with me again tomorrow."

Mama nodded "Well that sounds reasonable."

And so they did, for as long as Phyllis was enrolled in that school.

About that time Willie, sixteen, started living with Grandpa and Grandma Counts. His relationship with P.G. had not improved since their earlier confrontation in Weed, and he had little tolerance for their drinking.

Things weren't easy for Willie there. Grandpa was disabled from chronic asthma and Grandma did sewing alterations at a nice clothing store. With what Willie could contribute working at odd jobs, and what Murrel earned from playing fiddle in a band, they were able to get by. Most importantly, Willie didn't have to deal with P.G. and his parents' drinking.

After Willie left, we all moved from the motel to a small house in town. Mama and P.G. set their bed up in the living room. We were now a family of four kids and we shared the two small bedrooms, our mattresses placed directly on the floor. Along with the basics—a kitchen table and chairs, stove and refrigerator—this house had something we'd never enjoyed before: running water. Phyllis and Reita, now six and five, would not stop playing with the faucets. Although Jessie and I had to follow them around, at least it made it easier to lure them into the bathtub before bedtime.

Jessie and I looked after Reita and Phyllis at night while my parents worked in the café. They didn't have money to go to bars but occasionally drank some after closing. At times I grew weary of caring for my sisters, but I accepted my duties. We had no family life to speak of but did play with the Donaghe kids whose family had moved to Artesia from the mountains, too. Mainly our life consisted of caring for our siblings and waiting for our folks to bring leftovers from the café .Our life was one crisis after another that threatened our livelihood and created anxiety for our future. I was worried about what was going to happen to us but I never gave up hope that things would get better.

And there were joyful times: the dances where Murrel played in the band. We were allowed to accompany our folks—and best of all, Willie was usually there too. The dances were held in roller rinks, airport hangers and other big buildings with spacious floors. We would sit around the edge of the dance floor drinking soda pop and watching in awe. When we joined in the dancing we could forget the bleak circumstances of our lives. It was the closest I came to living out my movie fantasy.

Our folks worked long hours in the cafe. The business wasn't doing well, possibly because my folks had no experience in running a restaurant. They also had no funds to buy supplies in bulk. They finally had to give up the café business and we were forced to move into a cheaper house. P.G. finally found a small grocery store that would give us a few groceries on credit. When P.G.'s brother-in-law, Glen Gathings, encouraged him to come to northern New Mexico for work, it must have been a welcome invitation for my folks. It was hard for me because we left behind Willie, Murrel, and my grandparents.

I was twelve years old, in the sixth grade, and the school year was not yet over when we moved to Bloomfield. We were not enrolled there to finish that year of school, and I am sure our grades were affected the following year. This did not concern my parents because their main priority was just trying to make a living.

The oil boom had begun in northeastern New Mexico and P.G.'s first job was working on a drilling rig located in Gobernador near the site where the Navajo Dam would later be built. We moved to that isolated area to be near the rig on which P.G. worked. We set up a tent by an earth tank and water well that belonged to the drilling company. The tank was the water supply for their rigs and our source of water as well.

In that tent, our folk's bed sat on a frame with a storage space underneath. The kids bedding, which lay on the floor, was rolled up during the day and tied with rope. A blanket hung in the middle of the tent for privacy. A table and a wood cook stove filled the front of the tent. We had an old rug that covered the earth floor. Just outside in our "front yard" we tied a hammock between two large cedar trees. Competition for that hammock was fierce.

Mama kept the tent neat and the rug swept clean. She cooked beans every other day and supplemented them with potatoes, macaroni and tomatoes, and other canned goods.

The tiredness in her face would disappear when we drove bouncing over rough roads, into Bloomfield to buy groceries and do the laundry.

She also enjoyed our family fishing trips on the San Juan River on P.G.'s days off. Having the money and supplies to do these things eased her almost constant worries. But, as usual, these joyful outings were mired by excessive drinking. Once we went fishing with P.G.'s brother-in-law, Glen, and we rode in the back of the pickup while the adults sat up front. On the return trip, Glen, high from the beer they had drank all day, drove recklessly fast on the way home. We were terrified and yelled for him to stop. P.G. and Glen laughed while Mama threatened to kick his ass if he didn't slow down.

The area was pretty, with cedar trees, plateaus and beautiful rock formations. We actually enjoyed living there; certainly better than in any town. Jessie and I spent many hours walking, sitting, and just watching clouds form in the beautiful blue New Mexico skies.

I remember one afternoon especially, when we had been lying on our backs on a large sandstone bluff warmed by the sun. "Look at that dark blue sky pushing its way through the clouds," I said. "Ain't that a beautiful sight?"

"It sure is. I just wish old Sarge was still here to look at it," Jessie said. "I might just go stay with Daddy. Boy I would like to see him" His voice trembled with emotion.

I missed our dad, too, and I felt a pang of worry at the thought of losing my other brother, but for that afternoon I pushed that worry away.

On our way back to the tent we found a beautiful collie dog wandering loose. We guessed that some oil field worker had taken him to the rig and he had just wandered away.

"He is so pretty," Jess said as he stroked him. Obviously Jessie was in love again.

"Let's name him Ring," I said admiring his lovely white collar. A good replacement for Sarge, he started following Jessie everywhere. They shared many adventures together. One turned out to be a near catastrophe: Jessie was standing on the edge of a rock bluff with Ring who was leaping in the air snapping at flies. Ring made a great jump, lost his footing on the sandstone rock, and as Jessie watched in horror, slid off the edge of the bluff.

"Ring," Jessie screamed staring over the edge of the bluff. He could see Ring lying still on a ridge near the bottom. Heart pounding, Jessie worked his way to where Ring lay unconscious. With tears streaming down his face, he carried him back to the top and laid him down. Amazingly enough, Ring finally came to, licked Jessie's face, and followed him back to the tent.

That same summer Jessie turned fourteen. He was far from happy. He grumbled to me that he could not do anything to please P.G. and said Daddy would treat him better. His resentment manifested itself in obstinance bordering on rebellion. One day Jessie failed to chop the wood to cook supper, and Mama had to cut it herself.

"Why didn't you cut that wood like I asked you too?" P.G. asked when he came home from work exhausted, greasy, and in no mood for Jessie's excuses.

"Well I didn't get back from hunting rabbits soon enough and besides, I'm not a slave. If you don't want me here I'll just go stay with my real daddy."

"If you can't do what I tell you," P.G. said, "That's probably a damned good idea."

By mutual agreement, Jessie went to live with Daddy. The next time we went into Bloomfield for groceries, Jessie caught a bus to Estancia. He would stay with Daddy for the next four years. He cried when he left because he would miss us, and because he had to leave Ring. Phyllis and Reita had tears in their eyes as they waved goodbye to him. I felt a great loss as the bus pulled away, for now both of my brothers were gone.

P.G. worked on the rig only a short time before disaster struck. The rig collapsed, trapping him beneath a quarter ton of heavy metal. When the other workers finally pulled away the wreckage, they discovered P.G.'s hip was broken. He spent the rest of the summer laid up in the hospital at Farmington.

At the same time, there was a housing shortage created by the energy boom that inflated rental prices. We had little money but we still had the tent we had been living in. We noticed an old house on Broadway with a backyard shaded by large cottonwood trees.

Mama knocked on the door and introduced herself. "I'm Bee Anderson and my husband's laid up in the hospital 'til his broken hip mends and me and my girls need a place to pitch our tent 'til he gets well."

Harold and Rosemary Firstenburg lived there with their four kids. The Firstenburgs were from Arkansas and Harold worked at the local radio station. Harold took one look at us girls and Ring in the pickup and said, "That would be okay with me. All I ask is that you help with the water bill."

Mama was grateful. "Thanks very much we will more than pay our share." That was the beginning of a lasting friendship with the Firstenburgs.

After a few days, Mama explained, "Bertie, we can't get by on P.G.'s state comp check. I'm gonna have to go to work and you're gonna have to watch after the girls. I'll try to get a job so I'll be home at night. I don't want you by yourselves with just the dog for protection." So Ring and I took care of Phyllis and Reita while Mama worked in the Avalon Restaurant.

In order to contribute to the family income I babysat a few times for our landlady, Rosemary, who was pregnant. With the first money she paid me, I bought some fabric, embroidery thread, and ribbons and hand-stitched a baby dress for her baby. Tears came to her eyes when I handed her the gift. "Honey, you shouldn't have done this," she said. "You should have made something for yourself."

Actually she was right. All of us still had very little in clothing. In spite of our best efforts we all looked raggedy.

When P.G. finally got out of the hospital, Willie came to Farmington and helped us move back to Artesia so that P.G. could recuperate there. I started school in the seventh grade that fall.

P.G. couldn't work and he and Mama didn't have a job so they spent a lot of time in the old Smoke House Bar in Artesia with his cousin, Mattie Shockley. As with most people who drink a lot they often got in loud arguments. Those arguments always scared us because we didn't know if our folks would end up in the hospital or in jail, by the time it was all over. When they were out at night, it was up to me to take care of my sisters and see that they had supper and were ready for school the next morning. Phyllis and Reita, now seven and six, sometimes resented my supervision, and were depressed that our folks weren't around. As for me, at thirteen, I often felt put upon for having to do my parents' job while they went out drinking.

One day we were dropped off by the school bus and were not surprised that Mama and P.G were not home. We assumed correctly that they were at the bar with Mattie. When suppertime came, I heated a can of chili and we ate supper. The girls grew restless waiting for our folks. It was getting close to bedtime and I told Phyllis, "You need to get in there and take a bath and wash your hair."

"I don't want to wash my hair. You're not my boss."

"It's dirty and it needs washing," I argued.

"I'm not gonna do it, and you can't make me."

I grabbed her hair just as she jerked her head back. "Oh, you hurt me," she screamed, "I'm gonna tell Mama. She was still mad when our parents finally came home and met them at the door. "Mamma, Bertie pulled my hair, make her quit doin' that."

"I was just tryin' to get her to take her bath," I said. "Besides, her hair is dirty."

"Bertie, you didn't have to pull her hair, no matter what," Mama scolded.

P.G. said, "Bee, if she can't start being nicer to the girls she can just go live with her Daddy too."

I was stunned. I had never heard P.G. say anything like that. He had always bragged on me. It hurt. I felt he wanted to be rid of me just like he had driven away Jessie. It was obvious they had been fighting earlier and tension was still high. Before I could say anything else, Mama turned to him and glared.

"Bertie ain't goin' anyplace. She's stayin' right here." I didn't listen to the rest of the conversation but I had the feeling that perhaps P.G. was trying to get even for something they had argued over before they arrived home. I knew Mama liked to have me there to take care of Phyllis and Reita, but I also knew she loved me very much.

I ran to our room and was followed by Phyllis. She patted me as I lay on my bed. "Bertie," she whispered, "I don't want you to leave. Please don't leave."

When I woke the next morning, there was no more discussion of my leaving, but P.G.'s stinging words stayed with me although I knew Mama would always stand up for me.

It was around this time that Willie got married. He was only seventeen but he had been earning his own living since leaving Weed. Even so, Mama had to give her written consent for his marriage. She went with him and his future wife, Mary Jo, to the Justice of the Peace who performed the ceremony.

Willie would later say, although he and Mary Jo were in love, that if his home life had been decent, he might not have married so young for there was no unplanned pregnancy involved. It was a good thing he had always shouldered responsibility, for the marriage would certainly demand this and more. He worked hard and supported Mary Jo and the three children they would later have.

In the middle of the school term P.G. was released to go back to work. My folks moved back to the Farmington area; this time with a small trailer purchased with state compensation money from P.G.'s oil rig injury. I was allowed to stay with Grandma Counts in Artesia to finish the school year.

I loved living with her. She was always partial to me, made me feel special, and comforted me when she thought my folks were treating me unfairly. She had a great influence on my life, giving me self-confidence and self-esteem. Although she encouraged my siblings, she showered more attention on me.

Grandma also offered guidance and good advice. To make a point, she once said to me, "Bertie, a long time ago when a child was christened it was a tradition for the godparents to give a silver spoon as a gift, if they could afford it. A child born in a rich family did not have to wait. That's where the saying 'born with a silver spoon in their mouth' came from. Now the way I see it, Bertie, you never had any rich godparents, so instead of a silver spoon, I reckon you were born with a rusty spoon in your mouth. But that should not dictate the outcome of your life if you choose to change your fate and work toward that end."

She also used to tell me, "Bertie, you be a good girl. Don't be smokin', cussin', or drinkin'." You're too good for that. A female with a cigarette looks like a slut. Cussin' show's you ain't smart enough to say anything worthwhile and, well, you know what drinkin' does to people. You hold your head up high and make somethin' of yourself."

I believed every word she said.

Grandma proudly hung my fifth grade award-winning painting, ribbon and all. She encouraged my artistic talents and supported me in pursuing them. My father sent me a set of paints for Christmas that year. I loved them, and was disappointed when the paints and paint-by-number designs were all used up. Grandma bought me a few inexpensive drawing tablets and some pastel drawing chalk and I continued to work at my art. She bought me some tubes of fabric paint, made me a skirt and blouse out of plain white muslin and had me paint butterflies and flowers on them. I wore that outfit with pride. Her praise, attention and encouragement convinced me I could do anything I set my mind to and she is responsible for much of my success.

When school was out I begged to continue living with Grandma but Mama insisted I come to live with the family. I was disappointed and angry. P.G. and Mama continued drinking and living a turbulent life. As time went on, their drinking and fighting escalated to the point of where we feared physical confrontation and were helpless to stop it. Although it rarely came to that, the threat was always there. I finally realized that it was good that I was home to be with the girls and help stabilize their lives for they still needed me.

Chapter Fourteen

I had just turned fourteen when P.G. and Mama traded the small trailer for a tiny house in Bloomfield. The house had two rooms, an outside privy, and our only water was carried in buckets from the cistern. But it was surrounded by a fertile orchard that produced sweet apples and peaches. And I think what I loved most about that time was the feeling that, finally, we belonged to a place of our own. At least for those two years.

P.G. could never stand the responsibility of owning a place, and trailers offered him the comfort of feeling instantly *mobile*. P. G's employment, like most oil-field work, came in spurts. By this time in our lives, we'd all become used to *portability*. None of us were surprised when P.G. traded the house for a "newer" trailer that we moved to nearby Aztec and at least we had the consolation that the trailer did not appear as shabby as the tiny house. Because of our folks' drinking, and the fear that they might create a scene made inviting friends to our home out of the question.

I loved going to high school. It gave me the chance to reinvent myself and I took full advantage of the opportunity. I was determined to overcome my background. I was obsessed with it. In a period of four years I made cheerleader, majorette, homecoming queen attendant, carnival queen, and I even performed in class plays. My sewing ability came in handy and I designed and made my various uniforms and all my school clothes. I continued to draw and paint with cheap paper and pastel crayons and was proud to show off my efforts. I did a painting of the area with colorful sandstone formations and cedar-covered hills that my parents proudly tacked to the wall. I loved the lush valleys and farmland bordering the San Juan and Animas Rivers but never attempted to paint them. I just never knew where to start and had no confidence that I could capture their beauty.

I did everything I could to create a good self-image, and I made friends who have lasted a lifetime. I treasured my new popularity and vowed to maintain a sterling reputation. I was so successful in that regard that some students considered me prudish.

Mama had never discussed anything about sex with me other than repeatedly warning that men would say anything to have their way and that pregnancy was usually the results. I learned about the functions of the female body, including menstruation, from Wanda Gurley when we lived in Weed. Mama seemed relieved that I didn't ask for information when I asked for some sanitary napkins. When I started needing to wear a bra she handed me a couple and said, "I bought these for me and they're too little, maybe you would like to try them on." End of discussion.

In March of my freshman year, I became sick one day at school. I rode the school bus home and went straight to bed with a high fever. Months earlier, Willie and Mary Jo, had moved to Bloomfield so my brother could work in the oil fields, and they were living in a trailer on our property. Phyllis and Reita were worried about me and called Willie. When he came to check on me and saw how ill I was, he became very concerned. Because Mama and P.G. had not yet come home, Willie called the bar in Bloomfield. Through the haze of my fever, I listened as he spoke.

"Hello, is P.G. and Bee Anderson there?" he asked. "I need to speak with Bee." He sat quietly for a moment then I saw his body stiffen.

"What do you mean they're not there?" He began to shout, shaking with anger. "I know damned well they are, and if I have to, I'll come down there myself, and drag them home!"

A few moments later Mama came to the phone and it didn't take much to imagine her usual greeting.

"Hello, what's up?"

"You wouldn't have to ask if you'd been here when the kids came home from school." Willie said, his voice now ominously low. "Bertie is really sick. She needs to go to the hospital if you can tear yourselves away from the bar long enough. And you tell that damned barkeep if he ever lies to me again when I ask to talk to you it may be the last lie he ever tells." He almost slammed down the phone.

P.G. and Mama came home fast. When they saw how sick I was they drove me straight to the hospital in Farmington. This was the first time I had ever been to a doctor much less a hospital. Mama sat up with me all night offering comfort and stroking me when I stirred. I saw fear and concern on her face when she learned the next day that I was diagnosed with Polio. The year was 1954, and a few months later, the Salk vaccine would be approved for use.

Amazingly I experienced no paralysis and recovered remarkably well. I know Mama felt awful about not being there when I came home from school. She must have felt especially ashamed that Willie had to pull P.G. and her out of a bar to take me to the hospital. She loved Willie so much that his anger must have cut like a knife. He and Mary Jo lived in the area for about three years before moving back to Artesia. Oh, how I missed Willie.

I worked from the time I was in the tenth grade to pay for all my clothes, school supplies, lunches and dental care. My sisters were poorly dressed in clothes Mama and I made for them and they visited the dentist only when they had a tooth ache. I was more than used to my parents' indifference to my academic progress. I had no expectations that they would suddenly change. But I did get angry when they woke us up by coming home late in the night talking, sometimes arguing, and rattling around the small confines of the trailer house.

My little sisters were still in elementary school and more than once they were punished by teachers for falling asleep in class.

In spite of resenting the interruption of our sleep, their safe return was a relief because when they went out to bars we worried the long hours away waiting for their return. As we grew older the roles of parents and children were often reversed and we were forced to intervene in their fights, both verbal and physical. Our negative upbringing took its toll. Not one of us was unaffected by their behavior. Willie felt the need to escape into an early marriage and Jessie, who had come back to live with us, dropped out of school. I was ashamed and felt I had to be perfect to make up for the way we lived. Phyllis was insecure and becoming rebellious while Reita was anxious and clung to me like a vine. But in spite of the trouble and strife we loved our parents.

When we were younger we tended to blame P.G. for the drinking. It was not until we became adults that we could admit to mother's role in the matter. Over the years, Mama had made a half-hearted attempt at getting P.G. to cut back on his drinking, including running people off who were bad influences. But she would then sabotage her best efforts by joining him at the bar or taking a bartender's job where P.G. would spend too much time drinking, unable to resist temptation.

My folks never paid much attention to what we did in school. In many ways that was a relief because the last thing I wanted was to have P.G. turn up there half tipsy, which did happen on a couple occasions.

The summer before I was a senior in high school, there was a beauty contest sponsored by the local Aztec merchants. The clothing store where I worked sponsored me in the contest; not because I was particularly attractive, but because the old Italian who owned the store thought it would be good advertisement for his business. Mama never told us she thought we were pretty because she didn't want us to be vain, possibly because her parents taught her that vanity was a sin. She would have thought me conceited had I entered the contest on my own so I made it clear that was not the case.

"Mama, I'm entered in a beauty contest. I didn't do it myself, the store did."

"Well, I assume, you had to give your permission," she said.

"Well yeah," I was forced to admit.

She was not impressed. Such things were foolish and she never approved of women teetering around on high heels exhibiting female vanity. In fact the only time I ever knew Mama to make fun of someone was when she mimicked her sister-in-law. This sister-in-law was a small woman who wore high-heeled shoes and short skirts to better show off her legs. She also lathered on plenty of makeup, mascara and bright red lipstick on her very full lips; lips that Mama described as "looking like a horse's butt." She wore her hair 1940s-style, with the sides swept up in rolls, and the back hanging down, secured with barrettes. She smoked hand-rolled Bull Durhams that dangled from a fake ivory cigarette holder, and swished around with that holder extended between her ruby red manicured fingers, rolling her big, brown mascara dripping eyes, and speaking in a whiney pretentious voice.

We kids fell over laughing when Mama prissed around on her tiptoes, pursing her lips, raising one brow, waving an invisible cigarette.

"Now, honey," she mocked in a phony voice, "You know, I have to use this holder. I just can't stand that yellow nicotine staining my lily white fingers." Mama always got a laugh for her farcical derision. She didn't really dislike her sister-in-law but she detested her pretention.

Even though Mama wasn't pleased at having me in a beauty contest, she drove me to the event anyway. P.G. was working that evening, but his brother, Doyle, who had been drinking that day, insisted on going with us.

I could not see into the audience that evening. The bleachers were hidden in darkness and were even more obscured by the bright lights reflecting off the swimming pool. I couldn't see anything going on behind the lights. If I had, I would have immediately fled the scene. At the time, I was more concentrating on walking in my high-heeled shoes without stumbling. And I was worried that I might fall off the runway into the swimming pool. I could not swim and was terrified of deep water. I was also afraid that the red and white swimsuit I had bought at the clothing store that sponsored me might ride up in back and show more than I intended.

I later learned that while I was worried about drowning, Doyle was waving money around loudly trying to take bets that I would win.

"That Tracy girl's gonna win!" he shouted. Here's ten dollars that says so. Do I have any takers?"

Reita and Phyllis turned away pretending they didn't know him while Mama silently hoped the folly would soon end. She was seated by a lady whose daughter was one of the first contestants to walk the runway in her swimsuit. Earlier, this proud mother had nudged Mama. "Just wait 'til you see my daughter, she's the one with the beautiful blond hair and brown eyes. She's the third in line to walk in front of the judges." As her daughter walked down the runway, she turned to Mama again. "That's my daughter."

Mama nodded her head but didn't comment. Doyle had found no takers for his wager and had at last settled down, much to Phyllis's and Reita's relief.

I was near the last of the contestants to walk down the runway. I stood up, tugged at my swimsuit, and quickly walked in front of the judges. My face was frozen in a smile. I thought I heard a shrill, loud whistle from the audience and something about, "Here's my ten." Fortunately I kept my balance on my new high-heeled shoes. At the end of the contest, when they placed the sequin-crusted crown on my head, Mama turned to the lady and smugly said, "That's *my* daughter."

After the contest was over and I joined my family to go home, Phyllis and Reita were bubbling with excitement. "We knew you were going to win," Reita said happily.

"Yeah, and Uncle Doyle really thought so," Phyllis agreed.

"I just wished someone had taken my bet," Doyle grumbled.

"Did you hear how I shut that braggin' woman up? Mama asked. She quickly recounted her sarcastic remark. That was as close as she would come to saying she was proud of me. I was embarrassed by all of their behavior but secretly pleased that Mama had supported me in her roundabout way.

Mama was bartending on Main Street in Aztec when I was a senior in high school. I worked at Spencer's Drug Store on Main Street at the same time; my job was much more pleasant than Mama's. One day a terrible thing happened right before her eyes. There was a couple in Aztec who had some domestic problems that landed the husband in jail. The wife was an ugly heavyset woman whose face bore witness to her former occupation as a lady wrestler. Her nose was crooked and flattened from having been repeatedly broken and her hair hung in oily strings to her broad shoulders. From all accounts she was as tough as she looked and had lost very few matches during her career.

While her husband was locked up for a few months she took to driving by the jail with her new boyfriend, taunting, honking and waving as her husband looked out from the barred cell window.

Mama said of her behavior, which was common knowledge, "That woman may be mean but she's not too smart. You don't tease a mad dog just because he's tied up. He could get loose and bite you in the butt."

When he was finally released from jail, the man came into the bar while Mama was on shift, ordered a beer, and sauntered over by the entrance. The bar had swinging half-doors, like those in the old western movies. Nobody paid much attention to the husband as he stood by the door drinking his beer.

A little later, the ex-wrestler wife, with her new boyfriend, came into the bar, swaggered past the husband and took a booth at the back of the bar where they ordered and paid for a drink. She pointedly ignored her husband as the two drank and laughed. After finishing their drink they started walking toward the door. She walked by her husband as though he did not exist.

At that moment, he quickly stepped behind her and grabbed her with one arm. With the other, he reached around and nearly decapitated her with a large pocket knife he had hidden in his jacket. She died instantly, her face frozen in a mask of surprise. As she fell, she crashed though the swinging doors and her blood ran across the sidewalk and into the street.

As this horror was unfolding, P.G. and my sisters were walking up the street toward the bar to pick up Mama who was finishing her shift. Because of the crowd that had gathered, Reita said fortunately all she saw was the blood running across the sidewalk and into the gutter. This murder didn't seem to faze Mama very much.

"It's those quiet ones you have to look out for," she said. "I knew that bitch was askin' for trouble when she kept tauntin' him. I'd say she got what she asked for."

I loved school and only missed class when I was ill with polio and mumps. In my senior year, I was allowed to take the one and only elective art class offered by the Aztec High School. I was recognized as a good artist by the teacher and other students, and I even made the school annual as "Most Talented." But much more importantly, I knew I'd found my passion.

At school, I made sketches and passed them around the classes. I used my art skills in biology to get better grades by drawing frog anatomy and other science related subjects, and I also helped other students with their drawings. I was always the one called on to design and make posters, fliers, and other related art projects. I made good grades in high school and was a member of the National Honor Society. My grades were not high enough, however, to win me a scholarship to college. The only students who received scholarships were the most brilliant, or the best athletes. The school had no guidance counselors and I had no one to help me get the funds for a university education.

I resented the school system that offered me no assistance but enthusiastically helped secure scholarships for athletes. This perceived unfairness developed into anger as my hope of becoming an artist faded.

Because I was convinced that only a formal education could produce the desired results as far as becoming a professional artist and this was out of the question for me, I just gave up the idea for the next few years. I resigned myself to the fact that I would probably never be able to attend college and could see no way I could become a successful artist without a formal education. My dream of becoming a professional artist faded into bitter resignation of a bleak future. For the next six years I was so angry and disappointed I formed an emotional and creative block and could not do any artwork.

Bertie's sisters Reita 11, and Phyllis 12 about the time Bertie left home

Chapter Fifteen

Even as I spoke encouraging words to the students in a speech at my graduation, I was resigned to the fact that I would be unable to achieve my own goals. My loss of hope bred disappointment and despair greater than any I had ever experienced. With few options after graduation, I went to work in a bank. I still lived at home and home was as chaotic as ever.

I had dated Larry Stroup my last two years in high school. He was four years older than I and had come from Texas to work in the oilfields. He worked for the same company as P.G. Larry's politeness and courtesy impressed P.G. who introduced us. That Larry didn't drink or carouse appealed to me. He was also good looking, well- mannered, and he pursued me relentlessly.

Larry was not critical of my family and for that I was grateful. I was enamored with him, and I believed I was in love. I had reservations about marrying, but he would not agree to a long engagement and kept pressuring me to get married. At times our courtship turned turbulent because of his possessiveness and jealousy. I did not recognize his behavior as a warning sign of things to come. Instead, I chose or was naïve enough to believe we could make a good life together. Larry and I married a couple months after I graduated from high school. As I said my vows, I was hopeful that I had made a good decision. We moved into a small house in Aztec.

After I left home, my sisters missed me terribly because they had to deal with our parents' turmoil without me. Our bond was strong and even though I was married, my role as a caretaker had not changed and I could not abandon them.

Shortly after the wedding Larry and I were awakened in the middle of the night to find Mama and the girls at the door. I welcomed them but not without some embarrassment—my new mother-in-law was visiting us at the time. She was a devout Baptist and I feared she would beat a quick retreat to Texas. Much to her credit, whatever impression of my memorable family she took away with her, I never heard so much as a whisper.

We sat at the kitchen table while Mama and the girls recounted the events that had occurred earlier in the evening. As usual, P.G. had gone to the lounge where Mama was tending bar. While waiting for her to finish her shift, he drank a few too many beers.

"He got mad when I told him he had too much to drink," Mama said, as she reached for her pack of Kools. "He even accused me of likin' the people in the bar better than him!" She tapped the cigarette package and grasped the first one to poke out its menthol-tipped head. "I was so pissed off that I had a couple drinks myself when I got off work."

Mama lit her cigarette, and, in bits and pieces, she and my sisters filled us in on what happened next. Mama and P.G. had continued bickering after they arrived home.

While she was fixing something to eat, a struggle ensued in the tiny kitchen of the trailer. Even though P.G. knew from experience that in a physical confrontation Mama would strike first and ask questions later, he failed to use his best judgment. Thinking he had better take control of the situation, P.G. came from behind and grabbed Mama by her ponytail. He might as well have grabbed a tiger by the tail!

"Turn me loose, you bastard!" She twisted around to face him but was too close to strike a blow.

"I will if you'll admit you're wrong and stop bitchin' about what I drink!" Grunts and groans grew louder as they bumped into the cabinets and refrigerator.

"I'm not wrong. You drink too much. When I get loose I'll make you wish you had a drink!" She took a few sharp gasps of air. "You know not to pull my hair!"

With her arms wrapped around him, Mama clung to the back of his shirt. Rip! His old worn plaid shirt gave way. The pearl snaps in front had released their grip early on, leaving him with just the patched sleeves intact.

"Now look what you've done, tore up my best shirt."

"I'm gonna tear up more than your shirt! I'm gonna tear up your *ass* like a wild sow's nest!"

Locked in a bear hug they circled round and round, each unwilling to let go. Mama finally ended the monster dance in the middle of a whirl when she grabbed the handle of the aluminum coffee pot and whacked P.G. on the back of his head. The pot was badly bent and coffee grounds scattered across the kitchen.

Phyllis and Reita slept in bunk beds in a room just off the kitchen. "I was asleep," Phyllis said, tucking her hair behind her ear, "until some coffee grounds hit me in the face." She made no attempt to hide her disgust.

"I was already awake," Reita informed us proudly, caught up in the excitement of the tale. "I heard the ruckus from the beginnin'."

"You noticed he didn't want any more of me after I whacked him with that pot," Mama said, with a small half laugh. Evidently P.G.'s fighting spirit diminished faster than the lump on his head.

"We told Mama that we should just come to your house 'til things simmer down," Phyllis interrupted.

At the urging of the girls, Mama consented to stay at our house for the rest of the night. As usual when P.G. and Mama fought, a truce was soon to follow. Both would later laughingly recall P.G.'s remark when they were shopping for a replacement for the ruined coffee pot. "Bee," he pleaded, rubbing the knot on his head, "please get a smaller one this time."

A few months later my folks were in a terrible wreck and Mama was nearly killed. They were returning home from a night of dancing at the old Wagon Wheel Dance Hall outside of Aztec when it happened. There was no alcohol served there, so Reita and Phyllis went with them. Fortunately, the girls left the dance hall to spend the night with some friends so they were not with them when the wreck occurred.

Around midnight Jessie came running into our house without knocking, and startled us awake. "Larry, Bertie, get up!" he yelled. "P.G. and Mama have been in an awful wreck! Mama's hurt bad! We need to get to the hospital as fast as we can!" He was fighting hard to hold back tears.

On the way to the hospital Jessie told us more. "I come upon the wreck right after it happened. I recognized what was left of their Chevy pickup." They had bought this used 1953 pickup when a new one they bought was repossessed. "The ambulance was just pullin' away. I jumped out and ran to the people workin' the scene and asked what happened to the people in the wreck? I told 'em those are my folks!" His voice cracked. "The cop told me the woman went through the windshield; said it looked like she lost a lot of blood. He told me they were luckier than the kid that wrapped his car around them though. He said that kid was dead." Jessie hesitated, his breath catching as he sighed. "I came straight to your house, Bertie. It's not good and I'm sure scared."

Knowing P.G. usually did the driving, I immediately jumped to the conclusion that he was to blame. At the hospital, P.G. must have read the accusation written on my face as he tearfully explained what had happened. The police report later confirmed that the car that hit them was going over a hundred miles an hour when the driver either lost control or went to sleep at the wheel; he had just finished his night shift on a rig and was eager to get home. His car skidded sideways as he rounded a curve on a hill. P.G. saw the car sliding toward them, slowed down, and pulled the pickup toward the shoulder of the road. But he couldn't avoid the terrible collision, which left him with cuts, bruises and broken ribs.

The force of the impact propelled Mama through the windshield, and left her so badly lacerated she almost bled to death. One of her legs was broken and several of her ribs were cracked. Her beautiful face would be scarred for life.

As we arrived at the hospital Mama was being rushed into the operating room. Even though she was fading in and out of consciousness, she somehow recognized the sound of my footsteps as I ran toward her down the hall.

"Don't let her see me," she moaned weakly. "She must not see me like this!" They held me back as they rolled her into the operating room.

I was terrified she would die. All my life, just the thought of losing my mother would bring unbidden tears to my eyes. Facing the real possibility of her death, I cried unashamedly. Later, when I walked into the recovery room I recoiled in shock at the sight before me: blood oozed from the densely stitched wounds on her bruised and swollen face. I became dizzy, and, for the first time in my life, I fainted.

My folks eventually healed from their injuries, but the scars remained. They continued to behave like rebellious teenagers and we continued to behave like anxious parents.

A year after Larry and I were married, at age nineteen, I gave birth on August 7, 1959 to our first son, Monty, a beautiful blue eyed baby whom I loved more than I ever thought it possible to love anyone. I was happy to stay home with Monty his first three years. Looking back at those years, I realize I must have felt some loss, too, because I had given up pursuing my art. When Monty was small, I enjoyed drawing objects and animals for his entertainment and education but that was the extent of my artistic endeavors. And although my marriage to Larry was not going well, I was determined to give my child a better childhood than mine. With this commitment, divorce would never be an option.

In 1960, Mama turned forty-one and my folks moved to Hobbs, New Mexico. In Hobbs, Mama tended bar at a nightclub where her younger brother Murrel, now twenty-seven, played the fiddle. P.G. worked intermittently in the oilfields. Mama, P.G. and my sisters shared a house with Grandma and Murrel and his wife, Maggie.

The nightlife atmosphere fueled the turbulence in their lives and created a living hell for Phyllis and Reita who were fifteen and fourteen, respectively. When the nightclub closed down around one o'clock in the morning, Mama, P.G., Murrel and his wife Maggie, would come into the house making noise and sometimes Murrel would invite other musicians to jam and party until daylight. With the loss of sleep the girls had a hard time maintaining passing grades. P.G. worked for a brief time on an oil rig but the rest of the time he sat in the nightclub while Mama worked and after work she tipped a few herself. That's when arguments would start. In one instance a drunken fight broke out between P.G. and Murrel that ended with Murrel beating P.G. so badly that he required medical treatment. The girls were terrified and would later tell me that they were thinking of running away to come stay with me. But by far, the worst was yet to come.

P.G tried to shoot Micky, a musician in his twenties, for trying to persuade Phyllis to run away with him. Because they lived in close proximity to the nightclub with all manner of clientele, Grandma Counts kept her shotgun behind the front door for protection. Micky ignored P.G.'s warning to stay away from his teenage daughter. When Micky came to the house to get Phyllis, P.G. grabbed the gun and walked toward his car. If Mama had not grabbed the gun just as P.G. fired, the blast would have struck the man in the head instead of just shattering his car window. P.G. was thrown in jail until the judge set a date for the trial. The seriousness of their situation finally brought Mama and P.G. to their senses. They did not want to lose their daughters and in the nick of time had a real "come to Jesus moment." They made the decision to turn their lives around.

This change included a move to Delta, Colorado, in 1961 where, with the small insurance settlement for their injuries in the wreck, they made a down payment on a small place on Garnett Mesa. Delta, a farming community, was completely different from the New Mexico oilfields. Both parents liked living in Colorado. Once again, Mama stopped drinking and tried to get P.G. to do the same. Phyllis and Reita were happier and liked going to school in Delta; it was a better place for them to live.

On a visit to my folks, Larry and I fell in love with Colorado. Part of this love affair might have been the fact that I was overjoyed to find Mama and P.G. sober and leading a peaceful life—a life many families considered normal. But for us, normalcy was nothing to take for granted.

My parents were a pleasure to be around. They were farming their small property, raising a garden and had a horse and chickens. Phyllis and Reita were enjoying going to school and had made new friends.

When I found out I was pregnant again, I went to work briefly to earn money to help pay the expenses of having another baby. On May 30, 1962, I had my younger son, Kelly who added to the love in my life. My children became the light of my life—my reason for living. I was grateful for their love and blessed by their presence.

Larry had started a trucking business in Aztec but oilfield work in the area was in a slump and we were facing financial difficulties. Kelly was five days old when we moved to Delta. Larry got a job with the forest service, but he knew nothing about cleaning up logging areas. When that job failed, we were forced to declare bankruptcy and live with my folks for a few months.

Larry had a winning personality but it was around that time that I was forced to realize that Larry did not always tell the truth, especially with regard to business dealings and money. I turned a blind eye to this in the hope he would change but his lies sowed the seeds of disaster and were the beginning of real problems in our marriage.

When Kelly was three months old, I went to work to help make a living. Not wanting to leave my children in the care of strangers, I chose family members to care for them. I paid Mama to babysit although she would have done it for nothing. Comforted though I was that my boys were loved and cared for, I often left the house with tears in my eyes. I was envious of those mothers who did not have to work and could stay home with their babies.

My folks were better grandparents than they had been parents, maybe because they were older and more mature. They adored Monty and Kelly and though they still drank some, Mama never drank when the boys were in her care.

Larry was a good father when our sons were little and we spent every hour with them when we weren't working. We took them everywhere we went and treasured our time together.

The four of us moved back to New Mexico when Larry took a job checking wells in the oilfields. A few months later we went back to Colorado, where Larry managed a propane company in Hotchkiss. I returned to work for the school district office.

I loved the mountains in Western Colorado. Everywhere I looked I could visualize paintings from the beautiful scenery. There I began my return to art by taking a few lessons in oil painting from an elderly artist in Delta.

She inspired me to start drawing and painting again. A few years later, at a watercolor demonstration, I became infatuated with that medium, which is very seductive, and difficult to master. The challenge was irresistible. I was determined to learn more about it.

In 1964, at the age of forty-six, Daddy died of a heart attack brought on by diabetes. Larry and I drove to Estancia for his funeral. I handled the news of his death well until I saw his face as he lay in the casket. At that moment I was forced to accept that he was forever lost to me. My sorrow for a lifetime without him overwhelmed me. The infrequent letters and few short visits over the years were so inadequate. The wall of self-control tumbled and I wept for all the experiences I had missed.

Daddy had remarried, and I had a ten-year-old stepbrother, Joe. He and Jessie absolutely adored our father. My grief for the loss of Daddy could not compare to that of my brothers who had spent more time with him. Willie was sad too, because Daddy had always treated him like his own son. Years later I visited Joe and his family in California and found him to be a good man with a lovely family. His son was named for our father, Hollan Tracy.

It was at Daddy's funeral that I received one of the nicest compliments ever paid me. One of P.G.'s cousins, who attended the service, sought me out to tell me how she had looked forward to meeting me for a long time. She explained that P.G.'s family spoke highly of me, and had told her how diligently I had taken care of Phyllis and Reita when they were little. That unexpected compliment from a member of P.G.'s family meant a lot to me. Until then, I had no idea that my years as a surrogate mother had been noticed and appreciated.

Mama and P.G. had lived in Colorado just two years when they took on the responsibility of caring for Grandpa Counts during the last years of his life. Grandma had moved to Delta, rented a small house, and worked for a dry cleaning store. She had been separated from Grandpa, who lived in Albuquerque for the last five years and she had no interest in taking care of him. It was very difficult, but Mama, rising to the challenge, cleaned, fed, and nursed her father without complaint. To his credit, P.G. never once mentioned the inconvenience this care created.

During this time Mama's brother, Bill, often visited us. He had learned to make boots in prison and was working in a boot shop in Grand Junction. On Sundays, I usually cooked a big meal, gave haircuts to anyone needing them, and Bill would play his guitar and sing old cowboy ballads. Many of these songs came from a book Willie had found years ago in an old building in Hope, New Mexico. Bill had a beautiful voice, singing the ballads and reciting the poetry with conviction, for he had once been a cowboy.

P.G. especially enjoyed the family gatherings. He loved having people around. To him, the more, the merrier.

Even the sadness of Grandpa's declining health could not still the laughter of everyday life. Reita was now fifteen, with an exaggerated flare for drama that provided many good laughs. She was also endowed with overly bountiful bosoms, which at times, like unruly twins, garnered unwelcome attention, got in her way, and caused big problems.

One Saturday morning, after putting a pressure cooker of beans on the stove, Mama asked Reita to keep an eye on Grandpa while she weeded the garden. Although he was very ill, Grandpa liked to sit at the kitchen table with a cup of coffee. Because his false teeth fit poorly, Grandpa could not wear his upper plate and this caused his upper lip to flutter when he sipped.

He was at the table, as usual, and had just taken a fluttering sip when the valve on the pressure cooker suddenly blew off, loudly spewing bean juice and hulls onto the ceiling. The valve had plugged up, and the pressure had blown it out. Grandpa, although not splattered with hot bean juice, was startled and alarmed nonetheless.

Reita, in the bathroom, had just run a tub to take a bath. As she stuck her toe into the water to check the temperature, she heard Grandpa's loud, shaky voice from the adjacent kitchen.

"Come take care of this cooker," he yelled. "It's about to blow up!"

Reita, afraid that Grandpa was hurt, panicked and came running out of the bathroom into the kitchen. She was completely naked! Grandpa, seeing a naked Reita, was more horrified by this sight than any possibility of injury from the cooker. He responded as though she was a threat to his life!

"You naked little bitch!" he wheezed, his eyes round as silver dollars. "Get the hell out of here!"

Startled and shaken, Reita beat a fast retreat and slammed the bathroom door, catching her left "twin" as she did so. The house was filled with the crying and screaming of both Grandpa and Reita.

#

Mama and P.G. sold their Colorado place on Garnet Mesa because it was too small to make an adequate living. P.G. then began working on ranches. Being a cowboy suited him just fine and he was very good at it.

Mama worked right along side of him. She loved to ride. Their life on the ranches brought them face to face with winter wildlife in Colorado causing deep sympathy for the cold starved animals that replaced their enjoyment of hunting. Mama became an avid bird feeder.

Because P.G. worked on various ranches, my folks had to move into whatever old house came with the job. Without fail, those houses were dirty and riddled with mice. We all tried to help with cleaning the places and moving their belongings. We remembered all the shacks Mama had cleaned over the years and felt an obligation to lighten her load.

When P.G. hired out on the Columbine ranch northeast of Hotchkiss, he and Mama moved into a little old house that had been neglected and uninhabited for years. I helped Mama clean out the mouse droppings and other debris while Monty, eight, and Kelly, five, fished in a nearby stream.

As we were cleaning the little house, Mama, discovering a leak in the ceiling, climbed up onto the roof with some tar to patch it. Later, when she was mopping the floor below the patched spot, the sun-warmed tar softened, and dripped through the hole into her hair. With her extensively colorful vocabulary she described the tar in detail. "Son of a bitch! Would you look at this?" she hissed as she rubbed the black tar between her fingers. "That damned shit melted and is leaking on my damned head!" When Mama had finally exhausted her ranting she removed the tar with kerosene. After shampooing, her hair smelled faintly of acidic oil but it shined like a new dollar.

Chapter Sixteen

After Phyllis graduated from high school at eighteen, she fell in love with and married Bill Vaughn. Phyllis was so happy on her wedding day and beautiful in the dress I made for her that we did not foresee the heartbreak ahead of her. Bill would break her heart by becoming an alcoholic, cheating on her, and abandoning her and their two children, Clint, and Kammy.

Perhaps as a natural storyteller Reita had learned the value of colorful exaggeration, or perhaps her life really was more dramatic than most—either way, I enjoyed her interpretation of the things that she experienced.

Reita was a natural caregiver so it was no surprise when she chose a husband whom she could nurture and guide. Just as Phyllis had, she married at eighteen. Don Moreland, possessed juvenile tendencies that attracted her but were also an aggravation—not unlike her own father. Don was an avid sports fan who loved kids and dogs. He was also prone to accidents and Reita would often warn, "Don, stop bottle-assin' around, before you hurt yourself or someone else!" His infatuation with sports irritated Reita, especially when he watched ball games instead of making repairs around the house. Reita and Don would never have children.

Don's neglect in repairing their broken coal furnace resulted in a disaster that only Reita could turn into comedy-drama. At the time, Don was working at a dairy for a blind man living with his elderly parents, who had provided the small house as part of Don's job. The blind man was stingy and reluctant to spend money on repairs. In the middle of the night Reita and Don were awakened by smoke and coal dust as dense as Mt. Vesuvius ash. The dirty black cloud from the faulty furnace billowed throughout their house.

That morning when I went by their house to drop the boys off I was startled at the sight of my sister. Her eyes were red and her nose was running as she stood in the doorway with yellow rubber cleaning gloves and a grimy rag. Before I could say a word she launched into an angry tirade.

"I woke up in the middle of the night coughin' and gaspin'. I was afraid I was gonna strangle to death!" She rattled on stopping briefly to hack and cough. "It was black as pitch and I had to pound on Don to wake 'em up. We were covered in dust and soot! All I could see were the whites of his eyes and the imprint of our bodies on the sheets!" She bent forward, coughing. "If only he had fixed that damned furnace like he was supposed to, I wouldn't have to work like a slave to clean this oily crap off everything."

She took a deep gulp of the fresh morning air and continued. "As if that's not enough," she sputtered, "Don couldn't fix the damned furnace and our stingy landlord wouldn't call anyone to fix it for us. You know he's blind as a bat but that didn't stop 'em from tryin' to fix it himself." She cocked her head, pulled her lips into a grimace and batted her red eyes. "So what happened?" She asked, as if I would have any more idea than the Holstein cow that stood staring at us over the fence. Not waiting for nor expecting an answer she continued, "The blind bastard stuck his fingers into the fan blades and cut two of 'em off!" Her face was void of sympathy. "Now Don's gone to take him to the hospital and I'm left to clean up this mess! How's that for a night from hell?"

It always annoyed Reita when Don would watch sports nonstop on television, even during meals. One evening he sat mesmerized by a ball game on TV. His eyes were riveted on the action as he sat distractedly chewing and sawing at the steak on his plate. In glacial silence Reita watched his total disregard for the nice meal she had prepared. Don's neck was craned forward, his eyes locked in on the screen, when one misguided stroke of his knife sent his steak flying off the plate across the room.

"That's it!" Reita shouted as she slammed her napkin on the table and glared at Don. "If I had a football, basketball, and baseball, I would shove them all up your ass." Without taking his eyes off the screen, Don walked to his steak lying on the floor in front of the TV, picked it up, dusted it off, backed to the table and sat down. He continued eating as though nothing had happened.

Don loved dogs and always had several on hand. Reita hated these strays and the messes they made but was not unkind to them. One morning she called me at work upset and sobbing.

"Bertie, I've accidentally killed every damned dog on the place." A strangled hiccup interrupted her teary voice. "I was in a hurry to get to work, and I backed over that spotted bitch Don brought home last week. When it yelped I gunned the car forward and hit the white one—the one with the long legs and bent ear. I killed it on the spot." She snorted as she cleared her nose. "I was so upset! I yanked the car in reverse and backed over the spotted one again. That finished her off!"

"Reita, I'm so sorry." I said. "Just calm down, things can't be that bad."

"You're right." There was a slight pause as she weighed the situation. "That spotted one was an egg-suckin' son of a bitch anyway," she said dismissively, then went back to pleading, "But I need you to come help me get 'em out from under my car."

"I can't take off work." I said. "You'll have to get hold of yourself and take care of the situation."

"OK." Then click the phone went dead.

Her morning from hell continued. After pulling the dead dogs off to the side of the driveway, she drove down the hill from her house. She was still blinded by tears when two of the neighbor dogs, as they did every morning, ran out in front of her car. This morning, however, she didn't slow down for their challenge to the right-of-way. Her car bumper struck both dogs, sending them yelping and running for cover. Not stopping to see if they, too, were dead, she just continued driving and crying. As usual she got over her emotional hysteria, later recounting the story many times without shedding a single tear.

Larry and I didn't often go out when our sons were small. It was not until we lived in Hotchkiss and Larry joined the Elks Lodge that we started socializing. One Christmas we went with Don and Reita to the Elk's Charity Ball. A few hours into the party Don was more than a little tipsy. That did not sit well with Reita. She watched as he attempted to retrieve his jacket from a coat rack. She smirked, nudged me and motioned with a jerk of her head. "Look at Don, he can't find his coat."

We watched Don take what he thought was his coat, but instead, he picked a three-quarter-length woman's jacket the same color as his. Don tugged the coat over his broad shoulders, and looked puzzled at the tightness of the too small jacket. We were hooting with laughter. I began to feel sorry for him, but Reita was clearly enjoying his discomfort.

"Stop laughing at him, Reita. Can't you see he's confused?"

"Confused hell, he's drunk!"

Poor Don had no chance to correct his error before the owner of the coat marched up, and indignantly ripped her coat off him.

Although alcohol was never an issue with Reita, who was an occasional social drinker, she could never tolerate anyone drinking to excess the way our parents did.

We didn't see Willie often but after we moved to Colorado he came to visit us, usually to hunt elk on the Western Slope. We all looked forward to those visits as Willie, now in his late twenties, was still our most favored family member. We loved to listen to his stories; he was and still is a wonderful storyteller.

Most of the family accompanied Willie to hunting camp. He brought John Harris his old friend and boss with him a few times until John became too decrepit to go hunting. John, a big, raw-boned man, had a booming voice that was in part a reaction to his poor hearing.

The last time he came to Colorado to hunt with Willie he stayed in camp instead of trekking through the rough terrain. One morning after the other hunters had left; he was sitting on a small log by the campfire, peering through his rifle scope at the lovely mountain meadows. Suddenly, he was shocked to see three elk running straight at him.

Terrified, he fell backward off the log and accidentally discharged his rifle. He finally got to his knees, expecting to be run over by the stampeding elk. But he was astonished to see that the elk had slowed to a walk in the middle of the meadow at least a hundred yards away. He had forgotten that the animals appeared larger and closer when magnified by the scope. That was the last time John came to Colorado to hunt.

The next time Willie came to hunt we asked how John was doing. Willie shook his head and grinned. "Well, the poor old man's been sick and I finally convinced him to go the doctor the other day. Afterward, I took him by the drug store to pick up a prescription. It never occurred to me to go over the instructions with him and I didn't notice that the prescription was for rectal suppositories." Willie chuckled softly and readjusted his cap. "The next day, I noticed he looked worse than before he went to the doctor—all pasty and pale." He chuckled louder and longer this time. "I asked him, John ain't that medicine helpin' you any?" Willie laughed and finished his story. "It ain't worth a damned," old John groaned. "That medicine's awful. It would a done me just as much good if I'd stuck it up my ass."

At that point Willie stoked our good mood with a story about his Mexican friend who had shot his first deer earlier that year while hunting in New Mexico.

"Jose had just turned twenty and was so proud of his kill he could hardly stand it," Willie said. "He isn't a very big guy so we asked him how he planned on packing the deer carcass down off the mountain. He told us to help him just a little by hoisting the deer onto his shoulders so he could grab it by its legs and carry it off the mountain. He said he planned to stop and sit down on a stump or rock to rest along the way."

Willie shook his head and continued his story, "We lifted the deer onto Jose's shoulders and he stood there "bench-legged" under the weight of the deer." Demonstrating this stance, Willie stood with his feet spread apart and his knees slightly bent.

"Jose's plan might have worked except that he was standing with his back to the downhill side of the mountain. When the weight of his gun was added to that of the deer, the poor kid lost his balance and began flipping heels over head backward." Willie joined our laughter and continued, "He didn't turn loose of the gun or the deer and was able to regain his balance just long enough to shout *chingao!* before again flipping backward down the mountainside.

P.G. at work on ranch in Collbran, Coloado

Chapter Seventeen

We moved from Delta to Grand Junction in 1967 when Larry was offered a promotion with the propane company. At that time Grand Junction was a small town and an ideal place for raising our sons who were eight and five. Money was a major concern, so I immediately started looking for a job. I took Kelly with me as I drove around Grand Junction in search of work. He patiently waited in the lobby while I was hired by Union Carbide.

We enjoyed living in Grand Junction, which is surrounded by the beautiful red bluffs and rock formations of Colorado National Monument that runs along one side of the Colorado River. The Bookcliffs and Grand Mesa, with its lakes, aspen and spruce trees are visible from nearly anyplace in the town. Easy access to Colorado National Monument and Grand Mesa made living in Grand Junction a wonderful experience.

Living in this wonderful place, however, could not prevent the problems that were growing in our marriage. Larry's tendency to lie about small things that should not matter created mistrust on my part and anger on his when I confronted him. His jealousy that had been present from early in our relationship was also an issue. His jealousy began to manifest into anger. None of these problems ever really got settled—just smoothed over or ignored.

Although I was very busy working and raising two sons, I made time to do some oil painting. I joined a group of artists who shared the cost of live models and I continued to work on my drawing skills. I knew I had a long way to go to become a good artist and that it was solely up to me to make it happen. Now my passion was kindled and would eventually become a burning desire to succeed.

The family stayed close and I enjoyed the relationship with my sisters even after they were married. Just as laughter had helped us get through our bad childhood it also helped us deal with marriages that were not going so well.

Phyllis and Bill moved to Fruita, fifteen miles from Grand Junction. Reita and Don moved to Grand Junction where Reita worked in the St. Mary's Hospital Pharmacy. Their marriage ended in 1975.

Jessie lived in the area for a while before moving to Wyoming. After that he spent several years on the north slope of Alaska working on the installation of the Alaskan pipeline. P.G. and Mama continued to work on ranches for a time in Burns, Colorado and then in the Collbran area.

Not only did Reita inherit Mama's good looks, she also had her propensity for taking matters into her own hands. Reita was a small woman, but when she waded into a brawl her size never slowed her down for a minute.

Reita no longer worked for the hospital and for a while, managed a bar in Grand Junction. One day when an angry customer threatened his terrified wife with a knife, Reita went to their table.

"If you're gonna threaten your wife, and if she's dumb enough to listen, you'll have to take your argument outside." This ultimatum from a woman, and a small one at that, further enraged the man.

"Get your nose the hell out of our business," he hissed at Reita. "She's my wife and I'll do whatever I want."

Without hesitation, Reita reared back and decked him with a right hook. His chair tipped over backward sending him sprawling across the floor.

She stood over him, "You've got one more chance to get your ass outta here before I kick it out." He quickly left and his cowed wife followed. I learned of this astonishing incident much later from an eye witness who worked in my office. The family tended to keep such things from me.

During the time Reita was running the bar, "streaking" had become a popular fad of self expression. We were all brought up to be modest, but Reita was particularly opposed to public nakedness. One night she was startled by a flasher who came in the back door and ran through the bar, his white body glowing in the neon lights. As he started up a small staircase that connected the balcony to the dance floor, he tripped and fell. Reita ran to where he had fallen and kicked him with her booted foot. She dragged him across the dusty floor, a trail of butt-cheek tracks led to the back door.

My folks spent several years working on ranches near Collbran, Colorado, a beautiful little mountain village that sits on the north side of the Grand Mesa. At that time the town was a gathering center for the surrounding ranchers and farmers. On the weekends, we loved visiting our folks there to enjoy the scenery and small town atmosphere.

It was around this time that I met Gloria Tappan, who would become my best friend. Gloria and Tell Tappan had moved from Las Vegas, Nevada to Palisade, Colorado, where they bought a small peach orchard. Gloria worked for Union Carbide and we developed a friendship that has lasted longer than most marriages.

After a couple of years I felt our friendship was strong enough to introduce her to my family. I invited Gloria and Tell to visit the Collbran ranch where Mama and P.G. lived and worked. Gloria was delighted; Tell was reluctant. As he put it, "I don't want to spend the day bored senseless by some old folks." Boring? I wish!

The day we drove up Plateau Canyon toward Collbran, I became more and more nervous and apprehensive. After all, my folk's behavior in the past did not inspire much confidence.

Anxiously, I blurted out a last minute disclaimer, "I won't be responsible for any bad behavior of my folks. Sometimes they do some unexpected things." I was praying that for once, they would be low key.

Remarkably, Tell and Gloria liked P.G. and Mama immediately. We made it through lunch. But then my hopes for an uneventful "get to know you" were dashed when P.G., after playing the fiddle for his guests, tipped his recliner over backwards, and did a double back flip.

I was amused and amazed. Although my family did things that regular folks might consider outrageous, I found them humorous and loveable. I knew they were using humor to get through life.

Instead of being offended like I thought they would be, Tell and Gloria became friends with my folks. Soon, they met more of my relatives and were considered part of our family. Gloria and I have shared the good, the bad, and the ugly in our lives for the last forty years.

Larry's temper did not improve with time. What had once been sullen silences turned into frequent outbursts of temper tantrums. I tried to short circuit his anger by humoring and placating him. But this just made things worse. For years I pretended everything was all right and made excuses when he created scenes in front of friends and family. As I had done all my life, I tried to smooth bad situations over with the false hope they would get better.

I was determined my sons would have their father in their lives. I remembered Jessie's grief and longing for our daddy and I would go to any lengths to spare my boys that sorrow. Larry's good parenting skills when our sons were little did not extend to their teenage years and there were many unpleasant confrontations in our home. I became afraid of him and at my insistence we went for counseling. It was a failure. From personal experience I have found psychologists to be a waste of money.

During this turbulent time my greatest source of comfort was the love of my sons and working at my art.

I tried to keep Mama and P.G. from knowing the bad times I was facing as they had their hands full helping Phyllis through her divorce from Bill. P.G.'s sense of humor often masked his sensitivity to the pain suffered by those he loved. He was easily overwhelmed by their sorrow and turned to comedy for relief.

He and Mama were helping Phyllis move after her divorce was final. P.G. could not bear to see Phyllis so broken hearted and the thought of her little kids growing up without a dad made him cry. He dealt with the gravity of the situation the only way he knew how—drinking and comedy.

Reita and her second husband, Sam, were helping Mama and P.G. move Phyllis out of her house. Sam was a wannabe cowboy, who worked hard to give the impression that he had just moseyed in from the range.

In the process of loading Phyllis's possessions, P.G. spotted a box destined for the trash. He was pawing through the junk in the box when he spotted just the thing to lift his spirits from the bottom of their sorrowful pit. With a sly smile, he held an old shoulder-length blond wig up and closely inspected it. Fueled by possibilities his monkey mind kicked into overdrive. His eyes were red from crying, but when he stuck the wig on his head and topped it with his old cowboy hat, his face lifted. He looked happier—silly, but happier.

The others were used to P.G.'s antics and paid him little attention. He was disappointed that no one even giggled, and demanded to ride along when Reita and Sam made a trip to the grocery store. Once there, he assured them he would sit in the car while they went inside.

Sam, in his "cool cowhand" mode, stood talking with a man at the meat counter while Reita gathered up items from her list. As she reached for a bottle of *Mr. Clean*, she glanced down the aisle to see P.G. at the cash register in the stringy blond wig with red-rimmed eyes peering from under his cowboy hat.

The clerk took a step back, but managed to keep a straight face, acting like there was nothing out of the ordinary. Sam stopped in mid-sentence, and quickly headed for the door, ignoring the father-in-law who was tainting his cowboy image.

P.G. left the store frustrated that his attempt at comedy was unappreciated by the straight-faced clerk. But he visibly brightened outside the door when Reita started giggling.

Bee, helping P.G. on ranch in Collbran, Colorado

When my sons were growing up they loved to visit Mama and P.G. on the ranches where they worked. P.G., an overgrown kid himself, loved having them around. The kids followed him, helping where they could as he irrigated and did other chores. They especially liked it when they were allowed to ride horses. During their summer breaks from school I would pack their clothes and plenty of groceries and take them to visit for a week or two.

Phyllis was deeply affected by her divorce and afterward, Mama and P.G. helped her with her two children, Clint and Kammy. They too, liked to stay on the ranch with their grandparents. Clint told me that once when he was about eleven, he and P.G. went to Collbran and stopped in at a bar known as the D-Bar-J. Because P.G. drank too much to drive, he let Clint, who was eleven take the wheel back to the house.

"Granny" was so mad at Dadaw, Clint told me. "When he was gettin' out of the passenger side of the pickup and fell on the ground, she sicced his dogs on him. Old Zip, was a good cow dog, you know, and obeyed her. He may have thought Dadaw was playin' with him because he was down on his hands and knees. Anyway, Zip bit his ear and it bled. Dadaw begged Granny for help but she walked back to the house leavin' him to navigate on his own."

When P.G. was between ranch jobs, Mama occasionally tended bar at the D-Bar-J for extra money. Her job there created an opportunity for P.G. to drink even more and eventually lead to more trouble for them. Some of his jobs ended because the outfit sold or went out of business, but there were times when his excessive drinking resulted in his being let go. It is also undeniable that even though Mama controlled her drinking, she liked the bar atmosphere and never admitted that her bar tending contributed to P.G.'s drinking. She said more than once, "It doesn't matter whether I work in a bar or not, when he wants to, he's gonna drink." She would become angry that he could not control his drinking as she did her own.

I worried that P.G.'s drinking was risking whatever job he happened to have at the time. His periods on the wagon were brief reprieves. This pattern repeated itself over and over and I was helpless to stop it. We kids would just help P.G. and Mama pick up the pieces and move on to next job and place. In looking back, the burden of parenting my parents was taking its toll.

The D-Bar-J, owned by Loren and Bobby Wells, hosted an unusual crowd of regulars whose quirky appearance and behavior was a source of amusement. I once observed a woman, obviously drunk, who placed her false teeth on the table in front of her and was gumming a piece of the sack instead of the potato chips.

One day when Mama was tending bar she asked a disgruntled drunk to leave the bar. He was loudly blabbing of his exploits as a member of a brutal motorcycle gang. He became obnoxious and seriously pissed off at being kicked out. His rough pock-marked face turned bright red as he backed toward the door shaking his finger toward the bar.

"Come spring, me and my friends are comin' back here," he threatened, low and growling. His face twisted into a killer-dog grin as he glared at Loren, the owner of the bar. "We're gonna kill you, you red-haired bastard." Then turning to Mama and Bobbie, Loren's wife, "We'll rape the two of you," he threatened. Then he shifted his eyes toward P.G. who sat on a bar stool calmly nursing a Coors. "We won't hurt you, Pete," he reassured, almost kindly. "You're the only one around here worth a damned. Fact is, you're a fairly good guy." With that endorsement, he exited and was not seen again. The whole incident was forgotten until one day the next spring when we were visiting my folks at the ranch where they worked.

P.G. was looking through his binoculars across the mountain at the road and announced without emotion, "Bee, you better hide, here comes that motorcycle gang." Of course, there were no gang members, he just wanted to rile Mama.

Mama always held accountable those who wronged her or her children. If she felt it necessary, she meted out justice of her own. After Phyllis was divorced from Bill she lived in Collbran for a while. Also living in Collbran was a sorry lout who reputedly physically abused his mother and had gotten away with committing numerous petty crimes. This piece of human garbage made the mistake of attempting to rape Phyllis. He didn't know he had chosen to offend the wrong woman's daughter.

Phyllis foolishly accepted his offer of a ride at Collbran to Mama's house. After driving out of town he pulled to the side of the road and attempted to assault her. Phyllis escaped and ran to Mama's house. Upon seeing Phyllis's torn clothes and hysteria, Mama made plans to exact revenge and serve up some justice of her own.

Mama found out he planned to go to a dance the following Saturday night at the Vega Reservoir Lodge and made it her business to be there. She watched as he sat at a table sucking on a Coors and leering at the women on the dance floor. She sauntered toward him on the way to the ladies' room. As she walked by his chair, she swung her empty beer bottle at his head, connecting with a loud thump. He fell to the floor unconscious and bleeding and was later hauled off in an ambulance for some much needed patch work.

Mama went before the judge to answer to charges of assault on the man who attempted to rape Phyllis. She was forced to spin the story in her favor. Assuming her most demure look, she spoke quietly, giving the impression that she was just a vulnerable fifty-five-year-old woman.

"Judge, as I passed his table on the way to the ladies room" she lowered her lashes and hesitated. "He reached out and squeezed my behind." She then looked directly at the judge. "I swung the bottle without thinking; it was purely a reflex action."

The case against Mama was dismissed. The little creep did sneak around later and break the windshield out of Mama's car, but she took it in stride because she had extracted "her pound of flesh."

Mama dealt with awful situations fearlessly. When she was tending bar at the D-Bar-J, one of the regular customers, a young man named Tom Brooks, emotionless and automated-like, walked in with blood on his hands and clothes.

"Hello, Bee," he said in a flat voice. "Gimme a double shot of the usual." Mama poured a double shot of Jack Daniels and placed it in front of him. She sensed the worst.

"How ya doin' today, Tom?" she asked casually as she wiped the bar with a cloth.

Tom threw back his head and downed the drink in one swallow and motioned for another. "Bee, I just killed a bastard for beating my sister." He took a deep breath and continued in the same mirthless tone. "I told him over and over not to hurt her anymore and he just wouldn't listen. You know, she wasn't even married to him, she just let him live there." He shook his head from side to side. "I don't know why she put up with him for so long except she was just scared." His elbows rested on the bar as he laced his fingers together. "Well," he lifted one eyebrow, "she won't have to be scared anymore." He swirled the amber liquid in his glass. "He was still beatin' her when I walked in. So I just killed him." He looked directly at Mama with dull blue eyes. "Do you think I did the right thing?"

"I don't know, Tom." Mama sighed. "We do what we have to do sometimes." She picked up his glass. "Why don't you go back there and wash that blood off and I'll pour you another drink."

He nodded agreement, turned, and walked to the men's room. While he was gone Mama called Burt Chase, the City Marshall. "If you're lookin' for Tom Brooks, he's here at the bar. I don't think he's armed."

When I asked her later how she could stay so calm, she shrugged and said, "I didn't beat his sister, he had no bone to pick with me."

Mama didn't always escape the consequences of making rash decisions. At fifty-six, she should have had better judgment than to run away from home in the middle of the night. She was tending bar at the D-Bar-J, and not unexpectedly this led to P.G.'s drinking too much. She responded with anger. One night, after arguing with him, and having had more than a few shots herself, she made a flawed decision to just run away to New Mexico for a while. It was late in the night when she gathered a few duds and took a salary advance to go with the little nest egg she carried in her billfold. Her nest egg could accurately be called "mad" money—for she was livid!

She didn't bother to fill her '69 Chevy with gasoline as she angrily sped out through Grand Junction on her journey to New Mexico. She had owned the old car for a couple of years and had complete faith in its dependability. She drove with the determination of a greyhound chasing a mechanical rabbit through Montrose, Ridgeway, Ouray, Silverton, over Red Mountain,

Molas, and Coldbank passes. Late at night, as she drove through Durango she didn't see any service stations open. Finally she reached the isolated outskirts of the city and stopped at a station. There were no attendants, only an automated system requiring dollar bills in exchange for gas.

The instructions were frustrating and confusing and in trying to sort them out, Mama laid her billfold on the hood of the old Chevy. As she was trying to get the pump going, a van load of hippies pulled up, got out, and pulled a con game on her. One of them asked for directions while another grabbed her billfold off the hood. They then leapt back in the van and sped off.

Mama quickly opened the car door and grabbed her army-issue Colt 45 caliber semi-automatic pistol from beneath the seat. She whirled around and began firing at the van until the 9-shot clip was empty. She missed the tires but thought she saw sparks flying from the van. "I peppered the piss out of 'em," she would later recount.

When her anger subsided, bitter realization sank in. With no money, her run-away trip would have to be aborted. She fervently hoped that one of her bullets had hit its mark resulting in the death or, at the least, the wilting of a flower child.

"My fear was that the lice-infested, longhaired buggers had contacted the police," she confessed. "So the only alternative was to turn around and head back over the mountains toward home."

She was driving back through Durango when she saw a cop car and became paranoid, sure that he was going to pursue her. To evade capture, she raced as fast as the old Chevy would travel to a turnoff at Molas Lake, hiding in the shadow of trees for an hour or so until she was sure she had evaded the law.

I would never have learned of this escapade, except that Mama, penniless, was forced to call Reita to meet her in Ouray with gas money. She was humiliated to have been bested by the likes of filthy hippies and begged Reita not to tell anyone. Reita kept the secret for a couple years and Mama never told me about it, probably because she knew I might reprimand her.

Visiting my folks on the ranches they worked was sometimes relaxing and other times chaotic. It was sort of like Forrest Gump's box of candy "You never knew what you were going to get!" I took advantage of these visits to photograph and study animals, old barns and other scenery to paint.

Things got off to a bad start one morning when Gloria and I walked in and I realized Mama and P.G. already had a few beers under their belts. I was disappointed and did not hide my disapproval.

"What have you guys been doing?"

Mama turned rigid, looked me squarely in the face and cleared her throat. "I thought you'd *never* ask." This ended any further questioning on my part. I knew that it was not a good time to lecture on the finer points of sobriety.

Later in the evening a family fracas started when Phyllis's second husband, Howard, started picking on her. We intervened when their heated words threatened to turn into physical violence. Just when things seemed under control, P.G. jumped on the kitchen cabinet and dove through an open divider into the living room. Like a monkey, he landed on Howard's back and, with a mild chokehold, extracted an apology from him. I was mortified by the ridiculous exhibition. Tell and Gloria, amused, rooted for what they considered justice.

After things settled down, Mama proved to be far ahead of her time when she demonstrated how to serve potato chips.

"Do you have a bowl to put these chips in, I asked, holding a bag of Ruffle potato chips.

Mama grabbed the bag, ripped the top off, and dumped them on the table declaring, "This is the way you serve chips!" Years later I saw a TV commercial showing people serving chips in the same manner. Did they steal Mama's idea?

#

When a group of us went to the Cattlemen's Ball in Collbran, early on things got off on the wrong foot. Donna Helams, who owned the community building where the dance was held, had been a thorn in Mama's side for quite some time. Mama claimed that she openly flirted with P.G. many times in the past. The Cattlemen's Ball was an affair enjoyed by folks of all ages. No refreshments were served in the building and no alcohol was allowed inside. That evening, P.G., as was his custom, was dancing with every wallflower he could find because he wanted everybody to have a good time. Mama and Tell were dancing around the floor when Donna Helams grabbed Tell's leg with the boot that held a pint of whiskey—bootleg whiskey—if you will.

"What the hell are you grabbing at, Donna?" Mama challenged, turning loose of Tell.

"He's got whiskey in that boot!" Donna shouted. "I know he has, and I don't allow drinking in this building! It's my building and those are the rules!"

"Well, I've got some rules of my own," Mama informed her, "and one of 'em is you don't touch a man while I'm dancin' with him." The altercation continued out on the front porch where Jessie was restraining Mama from administering to Donna the overdue punishment she felt she deserved. Jessie yelled at Burt Chase, the town Marshal, "Get that woman outta here before I turn my Mama loose."

The skirmish was finally broken up and we decided to leave. With tempers still hot, things veered out of control again when Fred and his wife Red appeared on the scene. A couple months earlier Larry had fired Red, who was employed at our liquor store for an infraction that she and her husband denied having happened. Fred jumped on Larry proclaiming his wife's innocence. Larry was still recuperating from heart surgery and Jessie, who loved to fight, used the excuse of defending Larry to take on Fred in the muddy gutter.

Reita tried to intervene by swinging at Fred, only to miss him completely and connect squarely with Jessie's jaw. Tell then became involved trying to pull Jessie off Fred. I was disgusted with the fighting and got all muddy trying to make the whole bunch behave. Gloria got caught up in the excitement and informed Red, who was trying to get out of her car, "Keep your ass in the car. Don't make matters worse!" Red complied with Gloria's order, which helped defuse the situation.

When we finally started home I got mad all over again when the whole bunch started singing, "Where's Red and Fred's Dead." I swore I would never again go with them to the Cattlemen's Ball; and I never did.

#

Around this time, although my own marriage was in growing turmoil, with Larry's angry outbursts more frequent and volatile, I still tried to help intercede in my folks' problems. Gloria said it was like they were a little train that kept running off the tracks. I kept setting them back on and then they would take off again, full steam ahead, chugging out of control.

Their fights escalated along with P.G.'s drinking. He finally got completely out of hand and became a monumental pain in the ass. For the first time ever I sensed that Mama feared what he might do in his drunken state. He would not listen to her or Reita and became combative when they tried to reason with him. He had been on a two-week bender and had eaten so little during that time that he was very weak. Mama was drinking very little at the time, probably because of the seriousness of P.G.'s condition.

Mama was at her wits end. Because P.G. was more inclined to listen to me, she enlisted my help to get treatment for his alcoholism. She did not go with us to their house to get him because she figured her presence would only incite him. I took off work and met Reita, who lived in Mesa on her sheep ranch. We hoped to be able to convince P.G. to go to the Veterans' Hospital in Grand Junction. Imagine our surprise when he readily accepted the suggestion. I referred to his "drinking problem" when I approached him, saying he needed some help with it. He made no protests as Reita and I helped him from the couch out the door and into the car. We drove him to the hospital. When we arrived at the hospital the admitting nurse was the first one to use the term "alcoholic" when referring to his "drinking problem."

His sense of humor survived his broken condition and helped us through the heartbreak of checking him into the hospital. The admitting attendant held a clipboard and pen and she asked a series of what are known as "intake" questions.

"What denomination are you, Mr. Anderson?" He pretended not to understand and she repeated, "What church affiliation?" He looked at her through blurry eyes as he considered his answer.

"None," he responded in a sodden voice, "I'm a heathen." He expected a reaction to his lie, but got no response. He gave humor another try when she tried to find out if a doctor was following his case.

"Is anyone following you?" she asked.

He struggled to focus his eyes and shrugged his shoulders. "Just the cops!"

Reita, who had been saturated with pity for him, hurried to the hallway to hide her laughter.

The real test came when the lady explained that P.G. would have to sign the statement that he was seeking treatment for alcoholism. He did so without hesitation.

The three-week stay in the hospital to "dry out" was effective and P.G. remained sober for a few months. He did not swear off completely but he never again got completely out of hand with his drinking and Mama never worked in a bar again.

Chapter Eighteen

I was thirty-four in 1974 and still working as a secretary for Union Carbide, and still ignoring my artistic yearnings. Larry, thirty-eight, worked for the Fruita Co-op selling seed to area farmers. A persuasive salesman, he earned bonus trips to Hawaii, the Bahamas, and Mexico. His selling drive and edge, temperament, and smoking, also helped earn him a heart attack.

In spite of our tumultuous marriage, I still had feelings for him and tried my best to help him manage his health problems. After recuperating, he decided to start a business of his own—a liquor store in Fruita. With money I had saved, and in spite of deep reservations, I helped him open his business. We both kept our regular jobs and we hired employees to run the store during the day. At night and on weekends, Larry and I took turns manning shifts.

Larry was proud to be the owner of his own business and I viewed it as my duty to help him. Our sons, who were thirteen and sixteen, managed their share of household and outside chores responsibly. When I was scheduled to work at the store, I made sure that the meals were prepared in advance. I did the grocery shopping, house cleaning, laundry and kept books for the store. I was exhausted most of the time.

Larry's inability to control his temper continued to be an issue, and for years our life together was not peaceful. Five years after his heart attack Larry underwent bypass surgery. Hoping to avoid his angry outbursts, the boys and I tried to humor and placate him. Our attempts failed. At times he became so volatile we feared he would have another heart attack. At one point I secretly called his doctors, to ask if his bad temper could be a symptom of his heart disease. They assured me this was not the case.

Just as things smoothed out there would be another eruption. I could sometimes sense "hell on the horizon," but at other times, I was taken by surprise. Although Larry drank very little, when he did, it increased his volatility. His outbursts were timed for devastating effect; he let loose at parties, picnics, and other public events.

If I declined social invitations in an attempt to avoid embarrassment and shame, he was offended. When we did attend such events, and I managed to have fun, he often became jealous and stalked out.

Holidays were the worst. The whole family suffered from his rages, his sulking, and his emotional withdrawal.

Looking back, I now understand that I felt complete despair and helplessness during these intense emotional and physical confrontations. After these episodes, I would replace these feelings with hope —until the next time. All I was doing was storing up depression, one shelf at a time until the closet was dangerously close to full.

His behavior made it difficult for our sons to respect and love him. More than once, their intervention prevented Larry from physically harming me.

I stopped at the house one day on my way from Union Carbide to my shift at our liquor store. I wanted to check that the boys had something for supper before driving to Fruita. The day before, Larry and I had fought about an outstanding vet bill he claimed he had already paid. He did not like to be confronted when he told one of his many lies. I wrongly assumed he would get over it.

When I turned into our driveway, I noticed a sign on the lawn in front of our house that read, "House For Sale". Needless to say I was taken aback by this unexpected development. When I got to the liquor store, Larry was waiting for me. I feigned nonchalance and acted as if I were unconcerned.

"I notice you have the house for sale," I said casually. "How much are you asking for it?"

Larry tilted his head to one side, and with a smirk, asked just as casually, "Why? Have you got a buyer?"

Obviously he had anticipated my question and was prepared with the perfect answer. It worked. I stood there with my mouth hanging open. Later I thought about it and saw the humor in his elaborate plan to win a round in our ongoing battle.

The next day at work I laughed as I told Gloria the "For Sale" sign story. She was aware of Larry's temper and tears came to her eyes at the thought of my house being sold out from under me. "How can you laugh?" she said. "That's just awful!"

"Gloria, can't you appreciate the forethought that went into it? That's a great improvement over just loosing his temper and shouting."

I suppose my choice to laugh instead of cry—a skill my family had perfected for decades—was to take the easy way out.

For the next years I worked my regular forty-hour job then worked another twenty hours a week at the liquor store. These demands, as well as the duties of running our household, exhausted me. I finally realized I must get off my self-made treadmill or I would collapse. In looking back, I understand that I was already dealing with the onset of depression. It seemed no matter how well I performed, there was no lasting change for the better in my life.

I quit working in the liquor store but continued to keep the books. I used art as a lifeline and promised myself that I would use any extra time I had to learn to paint with watercolor. I signed up for some classes and I realized I did indeed have time after working my regular job to pursue my love of painting.

In addition to painting on my own I took a handful of workshops from people whose work I admired. One of those who inspired me was Joe Bohler, a nationally known Colorado artist. After watching him give a watercolor demonstration I was hooked on that medium. At the first opportunity I signed up for one of his workshops in Monument, Colorado. My efforts to learn more were rewarded and I could see rapid progress in my painting skills. I liked the results I was able to achieve with watercolor. It amazed me that without having had a formal education I could create lovely paintings.

Bertie, happy when she started winning awards

155

My biggest thrill was when I won my first of many "Best of Show" awards in 1979. I had won several first place awards in the two previous years, but this was my first "Best of Show!" All the hard work, failed efforts and aborted paintings seemed worth it. The trial and error technique I used to teach myself to paint seemed to be paying off. The first gallery to show my work was in Ouray. My work sold fairly well considering that I was just starting my art career. My sons were very proud of my paintings and thought I was a better artist than I actually was.

At about that time, one of my good friends, Jo Fultz, an artist and teacher, made a statement I should have considered more carefully. She said, "Bertie, if a creative person stifles the urge to use their creativity, it will eventually kill them." I would later realize how true that was.

I was never happy working as a secretary it was just a means to help make a living. Although I worked with some nice people who became lifelong friends, I felt suffocated and longed to be using my creativity full time. I was forty-one in 1981 and our sons had grown up. Monty had gone to college to become an engineer and Kelly was working at a gas refinery in Fruita. His decision to make a career in the refinery business proved to be a good one; he has always made a good living.

My marriage was continuing to unravel and Larry and I eventually separated for two months after he made such serious threats that my son Monty intervened on my behalf. Although we sought counseling, nothing seemed to work.

Meanwhile, I was falling deeply into depression.

This same year, I injured my neck while moving furniture. I lived in pain for the next five months until I finally had an operation to fuse two vertebras in my neck.

The physical pain compounded by a hellish marriage and a job that smothered my creativity fueled my depression until it became unbearable. I had to take sleeping pills in order to sleep, was exhausted during the day, and had to force myself to get out of bed to go to work. I lost my appetite for food and for life. I convinced myself that I was not a good artist and I stopped painting. I took refuge from my pain in thoughts of ending my life. I blamed God for everything. My situational depression had created a chemical imbalance. I sought relief from my family physician, which was a mistake because he prescribed the wrong antidepressant in the wrong dosage. Finally, I suffered a complete breakdown.

Chapter Nineteen

I did not recognize the warning signs of danger and death. This demon—a severe clinical depression—crept upon me with the stealth of a world-class thief. All my life whenever I had felt sorrow or despair, I had managed to talk and laugh my way out of it. This time was different. I was tired, angry, and cried a lot. I could not determine the source of my misery, but it felt as if my entire soul were engulfed in debilitating pain. I did not know that my situational depression had created a chemical imbalance that was responsible for my condition. This ignorance nearly cost me my life.

Because of this imbalance, I could not focus my thoughts or make accurate decisions. I had lost all perspective. I viewed everything as a negative, overwhelming circumstance, with which I was incapable of dealing. "Paralyzing influence" is an apt description because physical exhaustion is part of the package. Depression caused me to wrongly believe I had failed everyone—myself most of all. In reality this was not true, but this mentally and physically debilitating illness led me to believe that I was a hopeless, helpless failure, and that everyone would be better off if I weren't around. In attempts to analyze my worthiness I wrote lists of "good" versus "bad" attributes. My "bad" list was always the longest and included my menial dead-end job, my failing marriage, my lack of skill and expertise as an artist, my inability to fully financially support my sons—the list went on. I believed I was a fraud and a no account phony.

I intimated to my best friend, Gloria, that I was depressed. But I did not allow her to know the full extent of my illness. I did not share the truth with her or anyone else. I kept my tears, my agony, and my suicidal thoughts a secret. My outwardly happy and seemingly jovial nature somehow concealed the truth from everyone.

Finally, I decided to take action. The decision gave me some relief, and yet, at the same time I was overwhelmed with sadness that I would not live to celebrate my forty-third birthday. I was mourning my own death—but I could not comprehend the pain my death would bring to those who loved me. I would look at my family and think how I hated to leave them. But my next thought was always how much better off they would be without me. In hindsight, I am astounded that I could have harbored such distorted thinking, but I did.

There were practical matters to take care of. I disguised my interest as self-protection when I asked Jessie about the knock-down power of the .38 caliber handgun I owned. A couple weeks later, I carefully composed messages to everyone in my family and to Gloria apologizing for my imagined failures. I told them that I loved them and begged their forgiveness for what I was about to do. I kept these notes in my desk at work as I made my final plans.

Larry had grown tired of running our liquor store, a break-even proposition at best, and he wanted to be rid of it. We sold the business to our two employees and Larry took a job driving a truck.

On the evening of February 11, 1982, Larry was to leave on his second long-haul trip. Kelly was scheduled to work the night shift at the refinery, and Monty was out with friends. I saw this as my opportunity.

I went home after work, prepared a meal, and had dinner with Larry. He did not notice that I was operating mechanically. I wished him well on his trip and bid him goodbye.

After he left, I cleaned the kitchen. I left a copy of my life insurance (it had no suicide clause) on the kitchen counter, along with a note that the house payment had been made. I took a few sleeping pills to dull my senses, drank a couple shots of whiskey, retrieved the .38 revolver from the bedroom and walked to the car with tears streaming down my face.

I drove to our bank, which was located in a nearby strip mall. I made the house payment and deposited my check in the night depository. Still sobbing, I drove across the parking lot and parked in front of a clothing store that was closed for the night. That's where I sat for a while gently touching the pages of farewell messages to those I loved.

My face wet with tears, I picked up the gun and stepped outside the car. I pressed the muzzle to my heart and I looked to the Heavens as my finger tightened on the trigger.

No. This can't be. I can't be alive. I told you, God, I'm done with living. Those were my thoughts as I slowly became aware of the sharp smell of alcohol, betadine, and blood. I heard the strange beeping of machines, and squeezed my eyes shut against the bright overhead fluorescent lights in the Intensive Care Unit.

The last and only thing I remembered was standing outside my car in the mall parking lot, staring at the sky. I was crying and shouting at God, "Damn you! You're not going to do anything else to me!" In my tortured mind I blamed God for my despair. Those words were the only thing God willed me to remember before I pressed the muzzle of the gun to my heart and pulled the trigger.

With the realization that I was still breathing I cried and cursed. The terrible pain in my chest was almost nothing compared to the disappointment I felt at being alive. When I began pulling at the bandages and tubes, cursing and flailing, a nurse administered a sedative. I drifted away from the glare of lights over my hospital bed and fell back into a deep sleep.

The next time I woke I heard a familiar voice. "Bertie, its Mama."

I felt the strong hand I knew so well, gently holding mine. I opened my eyes to the anguished face of my mother. Her eyes were bruised and swollen from crying and exhaustion. They were filled with sadness and love; but not scorn—never scorn. Her face, still beautiful in spite of the old scars, was drawn and pale and her trembling lips turned down slightly at the corners. It must have taken all her strength, but she didn't cry.

I started to say something to try to explain why I tried to end my life but she stopped me.

"Hush now, sweetheart, I don't want to know why you did it. I'm just glad you're still here with me. Nothing else matters."

Knowing her, I believe she must have wanted me to save my energy for living.

Her compassion was intolerable. I felt I was deserving of nothing but contempt. In my mind I was a useless failure. Her horror and surprise at what I had attempted was concealed behind her mask of strength. Never would she tell me how I had hurt her and the others who loved me; only that she was grateful that I was alive and would do everything to keep me that way.

This woman whom I had wished many times would behave in a more conventional manner had once again proven to be the very person I needed in the worst hours of my life. I had long ago absolved her for the roll she played in making my earlier life so terrible.

The bullet missed my heart by one sixteenth of an inch—and, only because my heart contracted as the bullet passed by and then into my lung before exiting my back. Amazingly the bullet did not lodge in my body or destroy any vital organs.

The doctors considered my survival a miracle. Perhaps only I knew that it was divine intervention and that God determined it was not my time.

He made sure that I knew it was His will and His alone, that I survived. He erased any memory of what I had done about a thirty-minute period prior to my pulling the trigger. The only thing he did allow me to remember loud and clear was my screaming at him. By allowing me to remember only my defiant assertion, His message clearly was, "It's not up to you, Bertie. It was I who allowed you to live."

I would later understand the horror my family had to deal with when they learned of what I had done. The authorities failed to contact my family before giving my name and the story to the media. It was about 10:00 p.m. when I was discovered and the news was on the radio at 6:00 the next morning.

Monty had come home late that night and he had gone directly to bed. He was asleep when my sister-in-law, Betty, called to ask about me. He in turn, called Mama, and then he became hysterical when he tried to tell her what he had heard. Although Mama was stunned, she tried to calm him down and she agreed to go with him to the hospital to find out more about my condition. Monty then called Kelly, who was at work. Kelly could not believe the news but he hurried to the hospital. Finally, Monty called the trucking company and they contacted Larry.

The news traveled through the rest of my family like a wildfire through dry scrub until everyone knew but Jessie. He happened to be driving fifty miles out of Grand Junction on his way to work. When he heard the news on the radio, he nearly ran off the road.

Because of our troubled marriage, my family's first impulse was to blame Larry for the shooting. He was saved from their wrath when they found out he had been out of town. It was difficult for them to accept that I had done this horrible thing to myself. They were devastated and they kept watch at the hospital night and day until I was out of danger.

They told me later that they dealt with the long heartbreaking hours by trying to replace their tears with laughter. One night they were huddled in the hospital waiting room when a weary P.G. spotted an empty gurney standing in the hallway.

"Damn, I'm tired," he said, as he climbed upon the gurney and lay down.

Tell walked to where P.G. reclined, pulled out his pocket knife, and opened the blade.

"While you're here and handy Pete, I think I'll just give you a vasectomy," he said, laughing as he waved the knife in the air.

Just at that moment the elevator door opened and a nurse stared in horror at the sight before her. Her mouth, in the shape of a big zero, produced not a sound by the time the elevator doors closed. In a matter of seconds the door slid back open and she was still standing like a statue, sporting the same frozen look when she heard P.G. respond.

"That's O.K. by me if you'll let me return the favor."

As the elevator door closed for the last time, my family and friends gave in to fits of laughter.

Within a week after having the correctly prescribed medication, my brain chemistry regained equilibrium, and I could think clearly, and with proper perspective. For the first time in what felt like forever, I had relief from depression. Although the last six months were the worst, in looking back, my depression had been growing for several years.

My family and Gloria and Tell stood by me. It was difficult to convince them they were blameless for not recognizing the extent of my depression. Gloria, in particular, was laden with unwarranted guilt. I explained many times that my doctor said that it would not have made any difference how much people tried to reason with me; without the proper medication to correct my thought processes, nothing would have changed my mind. Not one of them chose to lecture or condemn me or deride me for my bad decision. Instead each one of them was overjoyed with thankfulness for my survival and showed complete unconditional love and support.

Tell stopped by the hospital every day on his way to work. To the bewilderment of the patient in the other hospital bed, he joked about how the wind was whistling through the bullet hole in my chest. She finally realized that we were making the best of a horrible situation.

While I was in the hospital, I avoided looking at the ugly wound in my chest. Instead I glanced away when the nurses changed my bandages. After I went home, however, I was forced to look. The first time I saw my reflection in the mirror I was stunned at the gaunt face staring back at me. I finally allowed my eyes to drift to the awful wound in my chest. I was horrified. The realization of what I had done nearly knocked me off my feet. I knew at that moment that my life would never be the same and that I would never again deceive myself and others about my emotional fragility. With that I started sobbing.

After eleven days of recovery, my reentrance into my working world and society at large was handled in the only way my background had taught me to deal with an overwhelming situation—with humor and grace. I did my best to put my coworkers at ease. There was a hushed silence as I walked into the office bent forward from the pain in my chest; my posture alone was a reminder of what I had done. Naturally everyone was uncomfortable and anxious in my presence.

"How are you, Bertie," one of my coworkers inquired nervously.

Resisting the urge to reassure her I had checked my gun at the door, I said, "I'm pretty good considering I lost the fight at the OK Corral."

My humor seemed to put everyone at ease.

The kindness shown me during this worse time of my life was overwhelming. I received many phone calls and cards wishing me well. I had expected everyone to shun me. I thought they would judge my suicide attempt to be an act of weakness. Instead, they told me how glad they were that I had survived. I have kept all the cards from well wishers and continue to read them from time to time. I am still touched by their outpouring of love and I treasure their acts of kindness offered at the lowest point of my life.

I have tried to use my experience with depression to help others suffering from this horrible illness. I encourage them to get professional help. I explain that it is no different than seeking treatment for any other dangerous and debilitating illness. I look forward to the time when information and knowledge will completely eradicate the stigma of mental illness.

I hoped that some good could come from the awful thing I went through. I still reach for that hope. Back then, it helped me make my decision to change my life and make the most of my second chance.

Chapter Twenty

After my breakdown I was fragile and vulnerable. I made it clear to Larry that I could no longer deal with his anger and disruptive behavior if our marriage was to survive. Larry agreed.

In spite of his assurances, three months later, on Kelly's birthday, Larry lost his temper. And after an ugly scene, we separated for good. I moved out and stayed with my folks for the rest of that year while the divorce was finalized and we sold our house.

After we finally split up, and to this day, my sons rarely discuss their father with me. His irrational behavior obviously damaged their relationship with him. In looking back, I am sorry that I allowed my determination to make the marriage work to exceed my judgment as to when to give up.

Larry pleaded for me to change my mind. When that didn't work, he tried to delay the process by every means, including suing me for alimony. He did not harass me by calling my folks house because he had a healthy respect for Mama, especially her impatience with people who posed a threat to her children. Larry had no desire to experience it firsthand.

P.G. and Mama were living in Grand Junction where P.G. was working on a horse ranch. I moved into the smaller bedroom of their two-bedroom house where I spent my extra time painting. I stored most of my belongings in Gloria's peach shed for a while. My folks, concerned with my well being, were glad I was living with them. It was good for me too as the intense drama of their old rowdy days was in the past.

For a few months I continued to work for Exxon but I spent every spare hour painting. When Exxon's oil shale project shut down and I refused a transfer, I was unemployed and could paint full time. This change salved my psyche and I began to heal. It wasn't just the antidepressants that were keeping my depression at bay; it was the creative juices that could now flow freely.

My folks were very attentive, practically overseeing every brush stroke, and Mama enthusiastically matted and framed each one of my watercolor paintings. They delighted in my progress. With each painting I was becoming a better artist.

When I had completed about twenty paintings, I shared a show with another artist at the Kimberly Gallery in Grand Junction. To my surprise and satisfaction, many of my paintings sold.

In March 1983, with a couple women friends, I went to Great Falls, Montana to the Charlie Russell Art Show and Auction. It was a wonderful experience and I was fascinated by the "Quick Draw" event that preceded the main auction. Twelve participating artists had forty-five minutes in which to complete a work of art. They worked in various mediums; oil, watercolor, pastel, clay, etc. Hundreds of people milled around watching them work while the clocked ticked. Their Quick Draw pieces were then auctioned to build momentum for the main auction. I was awed by the skill and confidence of these artists. Considering my mediocre skills at that time, I would never have imagined that eight years later, in 1991, for three years running I would be one of the artists in the Quick Draw.

One of the most memorable things that happened while I was living with my folks was when I learned about Mama's bowling calamity. Knowing nothing of her bowling history, I innocently suggested one evening that they might enjoy bowling with Reita and Sam. I wasn't prepared for Mama's angry reaction; her pleasant face transformed, her mouth pulled down by a scowl.

"I wouldn't go bowling if they gave me the damned joint," she said through clenched teeth.

I was stunned by her reaction, which seemed to come out of nowhere. From the way P.G. hid his snicker with his hand and rolled his eyes, I knew whatever it was would be good. After a bit of coaxing, I was treated to the story of what happened the year before, when Reita and Sam took them bowling for the first time in their lives.

Being a very physical woman, Mama loved to exhibit her strength. When it came her turn to bowl, she chose the heaviest ball on the rack. She jammed her fingers into holes that were obviously meant for smaller hands.

All eyes on her, she swaggered to the start line. Gripping the ball, she reared back, thinking she might just knock the wall out at the end of the bowling alley, perhaps demolish all the pins. Her mighty swing and too-snug grip, combined with the weight of the ball, pulled her head first bouncing and sliding several yards down the alley, peeling the skin from her chin and elbows.

When she finally got up, the ball was still attached to her fingers. Writhing in pain and fighting back tears, she screamed at those laughing on the sidelines.

"You can take this bowling shit and go to hell!" She freed her fingers from the ball and stormed out.

She was never much of a sports fan and would often say, "I wish they would take that damned sports stuff off TV." After her unhappy experience, bowling was at the top of her list of annoying sports.

Best friend, Gloria Tappan and Bertie a couple hours before wedding fight

For the most part, and much to my relief, my new life was uneventful. That is until my son Kelly's wedding day. Kelly and Marla were to be married in a small church. The reception would be held in their new home.

The day before the wedding incident occurred, Kelly, Clint, and P.G. were celebrating the upcoming occasion. Earlier that day they enjoyed a few beers. Kelly was driving the golf cart that P.G. used for irrigating on the ranch; Clint was riding shotgun; P.G. (or Dadaw as the grandkids called him) had the backseat to himself. In their levity, as they were driving along a canal bank, Clint glanced back to discover that Dadaw was no longer on the cart.

"Stop the damned cart," Clint yelled, "we've lost Dadaw." Kelly braked hard and backed up to find P.G. lying flat on his back. He had barely escaped a plunge into the canal.

The next day, the wedding went smoothly, and the celebration flowed over to the reception at Kelly's house, when I was forced out of retirement from my job as family peacekeeper once again. Ripples in this small pond of happiness appeared when Tell and my son Monty started slinging verbal pot shots at each other. Tell provoked Monty with a stinging comparison, "You're just like my boy, Randy." This was clearly not meant as a compliment. Randy was a con man and even Tell knew that. From that point, the tension increased in proportion to the consumption of "gorilla juice," which is punch spiked with alcohol. It was never clear who spiked the reception punch as no confession was ever offered.

Jessie's appearance at the reception only exacerbated the situation. He had not been there long when he exchanged words with Marla's father, Lynn, who had remarked on the size of Reita's overweight friend, Joanie. Petty bickering continued when Jessie defended her right to be fat. Jessie did not realize that Lynn's voice box had been replaced with a mechanical device. "Why don't you stand up and talk like a man," Jess challenged, in response to Lynn's suppressed speech. At that point, some of the other guests eased Jess outside. Soon thereafter the reception drew to a close and Kelly and Marla departed on their honeymoon. I organized a quick clean-up of the reception area, herded my bunch to the door before more fighting could take place, and bid goodbye to Kelly's new in-laws.

My family, along with Gloria and Tell, continued socializing at Reita's house. Mama, Grandma Counts, and Phyllis sat on the living room sofa, chatting with Phyllis's children, Clint and Kammy. Gloria and I were in the kitchen preparing refreshments. Jessie, Tell, Sam, and Monty were talking around the table.

The squabbling resurfaced when Tell and Monty once again began needling each other. What started as low rumblings, exploded into a melee that can only be described by dissecting the events, most of which were simultaneous. Tell and Monty's bickering resulted in them pushing each other over in their chairs.

Jessie eagerly jumped into the fray. Reita ran into the kitchen to break up the fracas and slapped Jessie in an effort to get him under control.

"Jessie, shut up and leave well enough alone!" she ordered.

"Don't do that, little sister!" Jessie said hotly, and then he slapped her with the same force she had used on him.

Then Sam intervened on the pretense of protecting Reita. "Damn you, don't you slap my wife!"

This was a move Jessie had longed for. He could not tolerate Sam and thought he was pretentious and lazy. He welcomed any opportunity to fight him. "You little phony, I've always wanted to kick your ass."

They started wrestling, and Reita, in an attempt to intervene, broke most of her long fingernails to the quick. Tell and Monty, realizing they were "up to their asses in alligators and fires of their own starting," forgot about their own feud while they tried to break up Sam and Jessie.

As they tried to separate the two men, the kitchen table collapsed and one of its legs went flying. Glass broke, scattering shards. Somebody bumped hard against the washer, knocking it so far out of place that the dryer toppled sideways. There was plenty of shouting, cursing, grunting and groaning as the group moved clumsily in mass toward the back door.

Earlier, when Mama saw Jessie was "on the fight," she had called his wife, Hope, to come get him. In the middle of the battle Hope arrived. She did her best to stop the fight by pleading with her husband, but he failed to respond. At that point Hope fell to the floor, pretending to faint.

"Jessie, for hell's sake, stop fighting and take care of your wife," I screamed. "She's fainted!"

"She can get up on her own," Jessie yelled back. "I'm gonna kick Sam Allen's ass." He grabbed Sam by the shirt and ripped the collar off. I finally helped Hope to her feet and got her out of the kitchen.

Mama rose from the couch, where she had been sitting with Grandma Counts. She was aiming to get control of Jessie. She caught him in a bear hug and dragged him to the front door.

Jessie reached up struggling to tear loose from her, but she kept her grip. At that point Monty entered the living room. He mistook Jessie's attempt to free himself as an attack on his grandmother.

Monty ran into the hallway off the living room hidden from the view of those in the living room and grabbed a long stick that Reita was using to prop up a banana tree in its pot. He ran back into the living room to rescue Mama from Jessie's pummeling and from her ringside seat on the couch, the only thing Grandma Counts could see was the end of the stick, which she mistook for a gun barrel. She didn't see who was holding the stick and in the confusion, she screamed, "My God, Sam Allen's got a gun." When Reita tried to take the stick from Monty she was accidentally jabbed hard in the belly.

In the meantime, P.G., who was decidedly wobbly himself, from his share of gorilla juice, decided to help get Jess under control; and, in joining the fray, bumped into the entertainment center. It fell on top of him with a crash.

Phyllis, who had also joined the efforts to control the mess, wound up with a bite mark on her shoulder and a footprint on her back. Remarkably

P.G. emerged from beneath the TV and entertainment center with no lasting injuries.

Jessie was finally shoved outside and Hope got him into the car and took him home. Reita's little dog was so terrified by the commotion that he ran in circles from room to room barking shrilly.

After the riot, we took inventory of the damage. The kitchen table had no legs, chairs lay strewn everywhere, and glass shards covered the floor. The living room was littered with the entertainment center equipment and Sam's shirt collar lay in the middle of the debris like a white flag of surrender. Gloria and I were in the kitchen crying and wringing our hands, washing dishes and hoping for some semblance of sanity to return, if only for a moment.

The day following the melee Gloria and I tearfully recounted the debacle on the telephone. After a while we stopped crying and apologizing for the bad behavior of others, and started laughing. I bought a new entertainment center for Reita, to replace the splintered one. Tell repaired the table and replaced the broken window glass while Grandma sat on the couch and continued to harp at him for his part in the whole affair. Reita found Sam's collar in the trash and sewed it back on his shirt. She cried for days and had to apply medication to her ruined fingernails.

Reita and Jess were estranged for a good twenty years as the result of this act of folly. They finally reconciled after Reita divorced Sam for a multitude of reasons, not the least of which was that he wouldn't hold a job. Because the divorce was less than amicable, brother and sister now shared a mutual dislike for Sam, the designated culprit.

I would have to say that my family's penchant for settling disputes with fists, not words, sorely tested my skills as peacekeeper.

Monty Stroup, Bertie's oldest son, as a young man of 25

Chapter Twenty-One

 I had lived with my folks for about a year, when I decided it was time to get on with my life. I was forty-three years old and twenty-four years of marriage had not prepared me for the single life. I prayed hard for someone with whom to share my life and on April Fool's Day 1983 my prayers were answered.

I had finished hanging my one-woman art exhibit of mostly landscapes, animals, and florals in the old Café Caravan Dinner Club in Grand Junction. It was late afternoon and the place was virtually empty. I ordered a beer at the bar and waited; my attention on the list I'd made of paintings in the show. I didn't notice the man sitting at the end of the bar until he said very politely, "Can I buy you a beer?"

He looked harmless enough, so I shrugged. "Yeah, I suppose so." With that bit of encouragement, he slid off his bar stool and walked over to introduce himself.

"I'm Mike Marah, what's your name?" He had a very distinctive voice that reminded me of Willie Nelson, one of my favorite singers. With that we started a conversation. I learned he had just gotten out of a brief but bad marriage and that he was in the earth moving business. When the band began their first set, he asked me to dance. I was delighted to discover that he was a good dancer and possessed a great sense of humor. We danced and laughed the night away. He called me the next morning to thank me for the nice evening and he asked if he could see me again.

For me it wasn't love at first sight and I'm glad of that. My affection grew as we continued to date. In the end, I could trust my judgment and my emotions. His straightforward honesty was very appealing. Within a couple months, my admiration had turned to trust, then love that deepened with the passage of time.

Mike made it clear that he intended to take care of me and protect me from anyone and anything. For the first time in my life I felt safe.

Mike was born and reared in Colorado, and his home is Cedaredge, where much of his family lives to this day. Mike has always been a hard worker and is honest to the point of bluntness. He has become my best art critic with accurate observations. At times, to spare my feelings, I might have preferred a little finesse, but it's rare to find someone who refuses to sugarcoat the truth.

A year after being with Mike my depression lifted and I was able to stop taking antidepressants. He helped me meet the illness head on. He encouraged me to pay more attention to my health and discouraged me from involving myself in the problems of others. My folks were saddened when I left them to move in with Mike, but they were grateful that I had found someone who loved me and was dedicated to my happiness and well being. We would marry the following year on February 27, 1984.

For a couple summers we lived in Durango. I was free to spend time exploring the mountains and enjoy scenery. It was especially exhilarating in the autumn, when the oaks turn every shade of brown, red and purple, and the aspens glow golden. The scenic region along with Durango's historic buildings, were also conducive to painting.

The Gallery that handled my work commissioned me to paint their landmark building as it may have appeared in the 1800s, when teams of horses and buggies traveled the streets. I enjoyed the challenge and turned out a nice painting.

I kept in close contact with my family, and although I remained concerned for their welfare, I no longer carried their burdens.

P.G. developed lung cancer in 1983 and underwent surgery that same year. He no longer worked on the horse ranch. Instead, my folks had moved to a small house in Palisade, Colorado where they worked for Gloria and Tell during their peach harvest. One morning before going to work in the peach sheds they were sitting at the breakfast table drinking coffee when P.G. looked out the window into the back yard. "Bee," he observed casually, "someone stole your ol' Chevy."

"You're shittin' me!" Her chair flew over backward as she raced to the door. "I guess I'll have to call the damned cops."

The police informed her that the '69 Chevy had already been found only a few miles from home abandoned by the side of the road. She called Gloria.

"I'm afoot, can you come get me? Some thievin' jackass stole my old Chevy but looks like they've located it up by the park."

Mama's anger flared as they approached the scene of the crime. She got out of Gloria's car and walked slowly around her Chevy, kicking the tires and muttering things best left to the imagination. The car was "trashed," in this case meaning that hamburger wrappers, wrinkled napkins, and Coke cups were strewn around the floor.

"Ma'am, this old Chevy looks good," the cop remarked, noting her agitated state. Then in a patronizing tone, "Are you trying to keep her in prime shape?"

"Keep her in prime shape?" Mama said, "Sir, right now I'm just tryin' to keep the son of a bitch!"

P.G. liked to reminisce about his own car stories. Years before, he'd been so successful in his insurance scam when he burned down the house in Weed, he'd decided to take another stab at larceny. This time his target was a newly purchased used two-toned Pontiac, a real lemon. He believed the insurance people who insured that car were just as guilty as the salesman who'd sold it to him. An attitude no doubt influenced by his mistrust of any man wearing a suit and low-cut shoes. After several futile attempts at repairing the yellow and green Pontiac, it began to weigh like a stone around his neck. Further repair qualified as water down a rat hole. The way P.G. figured it, the only way he could break even on his investment was to make certain the car was totaled. That way he could request full reimbursement.

His challenge was to wreck the car without suffering injuries. P.G. happened to possess enough imagination to meet the challenge. After minutes of contemplation, P.G. had his solution—he would roll it over a cliff.

There happened to be a steep and dangerous hill leading into Durango, Colorado on the road from Aztec, New Mexico. P.G. and Mama were living in Aztec at this time. Because of New Mexico's Blue Laws—laws that prohibited the sale of alcohol on Sundays—P.G. had taken the forty-five-minute drive many a weekend to reach Joe's Bar, on the Main Street of Durango. Now he had found the perfect incentive to mix pleasure and business—drive to Joe's, and on the way, dispose of the hated Pontiac. However, in his eagerness to get to Joe's Bar, P.G. was a little careless. His plan called for a roadside stop when he would pretend to pour transmission fluid into the Pontiac. He did so quickly, because his thirst was intensifying at an alarming rate. When the coast was clear, he kicked the car out of gear, slid out from behind the wheel, and slammed the door. Then he shoved the car toward the edge of the steep incline. In his haste, he failed to realize his jacket sleeve was caught in the door. By the time he realized his mistake, the car was headed over the hill. In his terror, he exerted superhuman strength, tearing the sleeve out of his coat, and literally saving himself by a thread. Hours later he was still celebrating at Joe's Bar.

But the piddling amount of the insurance settlement certainly wasn't worth the gamble of his life.

It was 1985, the year of the Oil Shale Bust, and the Western Slope of Colorado was economically depressed. We moved to California and stayed for four years while Mike continued to work in the earth moving business.

Unfortunately the metropolitan environment of Southern California dampened my creativity. I simply could not paint. I missed the rural and mountain area of Colorado. To fill my time, I kept books for Mike's business, sewed, went to the beach, and visited the many attractions around San Diego. I especially enjoyed the horse races in Delmar. The setting was beautiful and the horses even more so. We still went dancing a lot when we lived in California.

Kelly had moved his family to Los Angeles about the same time we moved to California so I was able to spend some time with them and bond with my grandchildren. I would drive to Los Angeles and spend the day playing with them, and sometimes stay all night. We took trips to the beach, the zoo, Marine World and Disneyland. When they stayed with me I sewed clothes for them and cherished every moment in their presence.

Kelly Stroup, Bertie's youngest son, as a young man of 25

Chapter Twenty-Two

*I*n 1985 my folks moved to Lovington, New Mexico to help take care of Grandma Counts and Mama's brother, Dick. Grandma was aging and fragile and Dick was bedridden with emphysema. When it became obvious they could no longer take care of one another, Willie moved them from Torreon, New Mexico, to Lovington to take care of them. Willie had been divorced from Mary Jo for several years; however, his second wife, Dianne, agreed to help him take care of them. When Willie and Dianne realized it was more than they could handle, my folks moved there to assist them. My folks had to live in a tiny camp trailer until Willie bought a place with two houses. But Mama didn't mind the inconvenience because she was near her favorite child.

Four years later, in 1989, while Mama was recuperating from a botched hip replacement, Grandma fell ill with pneumonia and had to be hospitalized. That was during the time we were living in California so I traveled from there to help. Soon after I arrived Uncle Dick had to be hospitalized; and, within weeks, finally gave up his long struggle with emphysema.

Grandma was grief stricken but still maintained a sense of humor. As she began dressing for the funeral she glanced at her flat little chest then back at the bra dangling from her bony old hands and shook her head.

"This thing would fit better on my knobby knees or elbows," she sighed.

I had made a dress for Grandma to thank her for the many clothes she made for me when I needed them most. It was a Robin's egg blue, her favorite color, with a beautiful lace collar. I was bewildered and a little hurt when she wouldn't wear the dress—even to Dick's funeral.

In 1989 our dear friend, Tell, was killed in a car accident. I flew from California to be with Gloria, and my folks and Reita came from New Mexico to comfort her as well.

Unfortunately for me, the week before, I had tried to rid myself of unwanted hair on my upper lip. I had not properly followed the instructions on the box of the electronic depilatory device and I wound up with a mustache of scabs. Although I tried to unsuccessfully hide it with makeup, I fooled nobody. As I greeted friends at the funeral I could only guess what strange disease they thought responsible for the condition of my upper lip. Gloria later confessed that laughing about "Bertie's mustache" and my family's presence were the only things that held her together during that awful time.

On March 23, 1990, at the age of ninety, I found out why Grandma Counts had not worn that beautiful dress I made for her many years earlier. She was saving it to wear to her own funeral.

In April, 1990, seven years after P.G. was operated on, his cancer returned. Shortly after that, because the economy was better, Mike and I moved back to Colorado from California and I made frequent trips to New Mexico during the next year. Because of his drinking and irresponsible actions in the past, I perceived my stepfather to be a weak person. I was surprised at the way he handled the news of his impending death, as well as the way he conducted himself in his last months of life. I felt badly that I had misjudged him.

I was there in Albuquerque the day the doctors pronounced his death sentence. My sisters and I were standing with Mama when the doctor delivered the results of their tests. Because he had always cried about things that happened to those he loved, we were expecting him to break down. Instead, we watched in surprise as P.G., who was holding his old cowboy hat in his right hand, slapped it lightly against his leg, shuffled his boot clad feet and looked straight into the doctor's eyes. "Well, thank you, sir," he said without flinching.

If he ever shed a tear it was in private. He started hoarding his money for Mama to use after his death. He made his own funeral arrangements and seemed to meet his fate without fear. I suspect this fearlessness may have been because he knew he had never deliberately hurt others, he craved no material things, and he had always been true to Mama and to his word.

In the last few months before he died, P.G. didn't complain about how he felt and he continued to display a sense of humor. I was there when he answered the phone and someone asked to speak to Dr. Bea Anderson. P.G. mischievously glanced at Mama, "You must have the wrong number, my Bee only went to the third grade."

While watching the Winter Olympics ice skating competition, P.G. turned to me and frowned. "How do they determine the winner? Is it based on who can hold the woman above his head, with his hand up her ass for the longest time without getting a hard on?" A few years later the Olympic Committee ruled that immodest maneuvers would no longer be allowed in competition. Obviously P.G. was ahead of the others in spotting this problem.

The doctors described to P.G. how the cancer would kill him by eating through the pulmonary artery, causing him to bleed to death. Sure enough, on March 11, 1991, as he was getting ready for bed one evening, he started hemorrhaging. He attempted to run outside to avoid bleeding on everything, but got only as far as the doorway before he dropped dead.

After Mike and I moved back to Colorado, I started painting again. As my skills improved and my work gained a following, I became the subject of several newspaper articles. At that time I was asked by various galleries to hang my work in solo shows. I also tried my hand at teaching workshops, and giving painting demonstrations. I was surprised to learn that I was a good teacher. I always tried to share as much information as I could with aspiring artists.

When I first started showing my paintings my greatest thrill was winning awards. As time went on I began to place more value on the appreciation of my clients who purchased my work. For me, that was the ultimate compliment and validation of my artistic gifts.

The more I have learned about the effect of color and shadow and light the more I enjoy the beauty that surrounds me. My friends tell me that I've taught them how to really "look" for subtle beauty, and this has given them a greater appreciation of art.

By 1991 I was confident enough to do the first of three Quick Draws at the Charlie Russell Art Show and Auction. As my fellow Quick Draw artists and I worked to complete a piece in the allotted forty-five minutes, the milling crowd of spectators felt to me like a herd of buffalo. I may have been confident, but I was also scared to death. Besides, I felt way out of my league. My determination, however, far outweighed my fear. There was no room for error as the work of the Quick Draw artists would be auctioned prior to—and as a warm-up for—the main auction. I painted as fast and as accurately as I could.

I chose a water scene because I could make clever use of the white paper, which ultimately represented ripples in the water. In the interest of saving time I had memorized the colors I would use and the order in which I would mix them. With this approach I produced a successful painting that fetched a nice bid at auction. I was so proud and I'd had so much fun that for the next two Quick Draws I took along Reita and some friends to share the experience.

One of my proudest moments was when I was accepted in the Rocky Mountain National Water Media Exhibition and discovered that my idol, Joe Bohler had work in that show.

Once again though, my painting had to take a backseat in 1993 when I was diagnosed with breast cancer.

It started when I discovered a lump in my right breast. I called this to the attention of my now former doctor. He totally ignored my concern, shrugging it off and suggesting the lump was probably a cyst that could be dealt with later.

Even though this same doctor had improperly treated my depression, I did not question his judgment. I was as ill-informed about the dangers of breast cancer as I had previously been about severe depression. Had I been knowledgeable, I would have demanded an immediate biopsy and, possibly, a lumpectomy. Instead, it was six months before I had my routine mammogram. At that time, I told the technician of the lump in my breast. I marked its location on a diagram for the examiner. Even with this information, they failed to detect the cancer.

A year from the time I initially told my doctor about the lump I was back in his office for a physical. He had forgotten my original complaint. When I asked him what he intended to do about the lump in my breast, the startled look on his face told me I was in deep trouble. He referred me to a surgeon for a biopsy. The surgeon was incredulous that the lump had been allowed to remain in my breast for a year. He did not mince words when he told me that should never have happened.

On the day of the biopsy, Mike and Gloria accompanied me to the doctor's office. I knew in my heart it was cancer. Thirty minutes after the procedure, the surgeon appeared to give me the results. The sad look on his face confirmed my intuition. The doctor was kind and empathetic, and he was also blunt: mine was an aggressive form of breast cancer. He didn't laugh when I jokingly asked if I needed a referral to Dr. Kevorkian.

Mike and Gloria were so stunned by the surgeon's diagnosis that neither could remember much of the conversation. I knew exactly what the surgeon had said.

I must undergo an immediate lumpectomy to remove the area around the biopsy, as well as the lymph nodes under my arm. Pathologists would determine if the cancer cells had metastasized. Depending on these results, a course of treatment would be determined.

After leaving the surgeon's office, I rode with Gloria back to her house in Palisade. Gloria was holding back tears and trying hard to hide her fear. I handled the awful news of having breast cancer with my family's greatest weapon—humor. It was obvious that at that moment we needed all the laughs we could muster.

En route, I asked her to stop at a drug store so that I could purchase some lotion and toothpaste. As we walked down the aisle of the drug store, I turned to Gloria and said, "With my future so uncertain, I really don't know whether to buy a little bitty bottle or the big economy size." Gloria was mortified and her mouth fell open. Then, in spite of everything, we started laughing. To this day we still laugh about the size of products we should purchase.

Reita and Mama came from New Mexico for the surgery. We spent the night after at Gloria's house waiting to hear the results. It was a difficult night to say the least. The next day, when the surgeon came in smiling, we stopped holding our collective breath. When he told us that the lymph nodes were free of cancer cells, we smothered him with hugs and kisses.

But because the cancer had been left to grow for a year I was advised that in terms of treatment I should go the full nine yards. I underwent radiation treatments that left me tired but still able to be my active self. The chemotherapy treatments were a different story. I had to endure six treatments, each three weeks apart. About the time I started to feel a little better, it was time for the next one. The treatments made my stomach feel raw and it hurt all the time. Painful sore developed on the inside of my mouth, and just looking at the IV and needle before treatments would make my stomach churn. When I took my final chemo treatment, I knew why it had to be the last. I don't believe I could have survived another one.

I only cried a couple of times during the whole experience—and I admit I surprised myself. I credit Mike for not allowing me to sink into self-pity. He would point to others who were worse off. As I became bald we laughed that I was looking more like Mike every day. Again, God was watching over me and helped me through radiation, chemotherapy, baldness, and sickness.

In spite of dealing with breast cancer I was able to paint and sell many paintings during that rough year. I've had a clean bill of health since the treatments and I believe that, when it is my time to go, it won't be from cancer.

Following my recovery, I met Bonnie Iris, an artist who, at that time, was also a writer and editor for *Watercolor* magazine. I was delivering paintings to the Art Center in the beautiful village of Redstone, Colorado, when Bonnie approached. She explained she wanted to do an article on my work for the magazine, *Watercolor*, a subsidiary of American Artist Magazine. I was thrilled and I had the pleasure of working with Bonnie, who wrote, "Spring Comes to the Rockies." The article, in which I illustrated how to paint landscapes, was published in the 1995 spring issue. In the 1999 fall issue of *Watercolor*, my work was included in the article, "The Figure in Context."

Chapter Twenty-Three

*M*ama lived for ten years after P.G. died. She missed him terribly and took comfort in having her kids nearby. During that time she also lost her remaining two brothers, Bill and Murrel. Bill died of a heart attack. Murrel had succumbed to alcoholism and committed suicide. Only her sister, Virginia, outlived her.

Every chance I got I visited Mama in New Mexico. I knew she looked forward to our time together. She had long since lost most of her "fight." She'd become more subdued and she took comfort in her religious convictions. She even started attending church! She laughed when I told her she got nice "just in time to squeeze under Heaven's gate."

The most difficult thing I ever did was caring for her at the end of her life. Not because of the physical demands, it was my privilege to attend to those, but because her illness robbed her of all she had stood for.

My mama had always kept her fears to herself. However reckless she could be, she had always shared her courage with others. For me, that made her helplessness all the more unbearable. Like other members of her family, she had developed emphysema. I stayed by her side night and day as she deteriorated. The sight of this once vivacious, wildly independent woman reduced to a husk of her old self would forever haunt my memory.

Again and again she reached for my hand, whispering, "Bertie, I don't know what I'd do without you." Even as she was slipping away, I preferred to think of her as that sturdy, strong-willed woman I called Mama.

Epilogue

*W*hen I started writing this memoir, all of my siblings were still alive. Unfortunately, Phyllis passed away on May 18, 2008. After a long struggle with multiple sclerosis and emphysema, she contracted MRSA, a deadly strep infection. She had been living alone in a small house on her son's property in Paonia, Colorado for the last five years of her life. I was by her side until about thirty minutes before she passed away. It broke my heart to say goodbye. After all, I was more than a sister to her. It was like losing one of my own children.

Jessie, who stood by his wife, Hope, in her battle against cancer died of a heart attack the day after Christmas on December 26, 2008. I was grateful that I had the opportunity to read to him from my manuscript a few weeks before he passed away. He especially liked the parts where he was included in the story.

Willie still lives in Lovington, New Mexico with his wife, Dianne, and has been my greatest source of information and encouragement. His life work as a welder has resulted in him suffering from emphysema too. He makes beautiful fiddles and still enjoys playing music, and I, of course, still think he hung the moon.

Reita lives in Ft. Sumner, New Mexico with her husband, Don Wahe. She was County Clerk for ten years and is now employed with an agriultural institute in Clovis, New Mexico. We still enjoy a very close relationship.

Many wonderful things continue to encourage me to paint. I am always flattered when people enjoy my work and collect it for their pleasure or to hand down to their children. I am glad I can share my gift.

I find joy in painting all subject matter. To me, an elderly person's wrinkles, age spots, and sagging eyelids reveal a life filled with unique experiences. Understanding this makes me feel connected to them as I try to create a truthful image that I hope will be viewed as beautiful—warts and all. I try to capture what has taken years to produce. Sort of like painting a beautiful old tree with gnarls and knots. When painting a cottonwood tree, in particular, the tiny hanging-down white branches bring to mind the beard of an old man. I paint the tree with the same respect and pleasure that I paint an old person and think of how much time it takes to produce such aged beauty.

When I paint a child or baby, I especially love to paint their hands and feet. I can just imagine washing their tiny limbs and feeling how soft they are. It is a pleasure to reproduce on paper God's greatest creation. Painting their eyes is particularly engaging, because the whites are so clear and they have that sparkle of youth. Putting a rosy glow on their plump cheeks is like making a sick child well. My heart *smiles* all the while I am creating an image of them—I know that is so, because I can feel my chest expand.

When I paint water, I try to make the rocks look wet and try to imagine the sound of the water as it gurgles along. I make my brush strokes dance to the images of the noise of the rushing water. I move the brush in the same way the water swirls. Amazingly, the swirling motion works to make real looking water. The gift God gave me has enabled me to take that rusty spoon I was born with and replace it with a silver spoon of happiness, success and an appreciation for everything that has happened in my life.

Reita, Bertie's baby sister, on blanket at Walsom Place

Gallery

Stormy feeding chickens

Geese in shallow water

Swaping stories

Navaho grandmothers

Crystal River

Chair Mountain

Chicken Conference

About the Author

Bertie was born in Estancia, New Mexico in 1939 and lived her early life in various areas of the state. In 1962 she moved to Western Colorado. The influence of these colorful areas is reflected in her paintings which are included in many private and corporate collections.

She has become a nationally recognized artist with her work twice featured in the American artist's magazine, *Watercolor*.

Born With a Rusty Spoon," is her first book.

LaVergne, TN USA
17 November 2010
205217LV00002B/5/P